A Seat at the Table: Ethel Ray Nance & the Harlem Renaissance

Karen Felecia Nance

Copyright © 2025

All Rights Reserved

ISBN:

Dedication

This book, *A Seat at the Table: Ethel Ray Nance & the Harlem Renaissance*, is dedicated with love, honor, and gratitude to my beloved Aunt Marie Scott Nance, a remarkable woman who celebrated her 90th birthday in 2024. Her milestone coincided with the 90th anniversary of the iconic Apollo Theatre, a symbol of artistic excellence and cultural heritage that resonates deeply with the themes of this book.

Marie Scott Nance's 90th Birthday 2024

Aunt Marie's life is a testament to resilience, grace, and an unwavering commitment to preserving the legacies of those who have paved the way for justice, equity, and cultural enrichment. She was married to Glenn Ray Nance, the devoted son of Ethel Ray Nance, and affectionately called Ethel "Mom." Through her marriage, Aunt Marie became a part of a family whose history and contributions continue to inspire generations. Her stories and experiences are invaluable treasures that bridge the past and present, connecting us to the vibrant legacy of Ethel Ray Nance and her profound impact on history.

One of the most extraordinary aspects of Aunt Marie's life was her intimate connection to Ethel Ray Nance's home at 505 Cole Street in San Francisco, California. This home was not just a residence but a sanctuary of activism, intellect, and artistry. Aunt Marie and Uncle Glenn lived in this historic home and were thus able to witness firsthand the comings and goings of the history makers of the time. It was a place where the presence of luminaries like Maya Angelou and Dr. W.E.B. Du Bois was as natural as the sunlight streaming through the windows. Aunt Marie bore witness to these gatherings, where ideas were exchanged, strategies were forged, and the seeds of change were planted. Her memories of these moments are a testament to the enduring power of community and collaboration in the fight for civil rights and social justice.

In April 2024, Aunt Marie traveled to Duluth, Minnesota, to honor Ethel Ray Nance's 125th birthday. This celebration was not merely a commemoration of a well-lived life but a reaffirmation of the values Ethel stood for: courage, perseverance, and the relentless pursuit of equality. Aunt Marie's presence at the event was a bridge between generations, as she shared her memories and insights with Duluth's schoolchildren, elders, church congregations, and community members. Her stories brought Ethel's legacy to life, inspiring all who had the privilege of hearing her speak.

Aunt Marie's reflections during the Duluth celebration painted a vivid picture of Ethel Ray Nance's multifaceted life. She spoke of Ethel's groundbreaking achievements as the first Black stenographer and policewoman in Minnesota and her tireless work to address injustices, including her role in organizing the Duluth chapter of the NAACP in the wake of the 1920 lynchings. Aunt Marie's anecdotes illuminated Ethel's unwavering dedication to uplifting her community and ensuring that the voices of the marginalized were heard.

In recounting her memories of 505 Cole Street, Aunt Marie also shared stories of how Ethel's home served as a hub of intellectual and cultural activity. It was a place where the spirit of the Harlem Renaissance lived, even on the West Coast. Aunt Marie described evenings filled with lively discussions, impromptu performances, and a sense of camaraderie that transcended barriers. These gatherings were a microcosm of the larger movement that Ethel had been a part of in Harlem, where she worked alongside luminaries such as Langston Hughes, Zora Neale Hurston, and Regina Anderson Andrews.

Aunt Marie's dedication to preserving Ethel's legacy extends beyond storytelling. She has been a steadfast advocate for ensuring that Ethel's contributions are recognized and celebrated. Her efforts have included supporting educational initiatives, participating in community events, and sharing her insights with scholars and historians. Aunt Marie's commitment to this work reflects her deep understanding of the importance of history and the need to honor those who have come before us.

This dedication is not only a tribute to Aunt Marie's extraordinary life and contributions but also an acknowledgment of the vital role she has played in keeping Ethel Ray Nance's legacy alive. Through her words and actions, Aunt Marie has shown us the power of storytelling, the importance of preserving our history, and the enduring impact of one person's commitment to justice and equity.

As I reflect on the profound influence Aunt Marie has had on my life and on this book, I am reminded of the interconnectedness of our stories and the ways in which our lives are shaped by those who came before us. Aunt Marie's journey is a testament to the strength and resilience of Black women, who have often been the unsung heroes of history. Her wisdom, grace, and unwavering commitment to truth and justice are qualities that I aspire to emulate.

In dedicating this book to Aunt Marie Scott Nance, I also honor the broader legacy of the Nance family and their contributions to the fight for civil rights and social justice. Ethel Ray Nance's life and work are a central theme of this book, and Aunt Marie's role in preserving and sharing that legacy is a reminder of the power of intergenerational storytelling. Through her efforts, the stories of Ethel Ray Nance and the Harlem Renaissance continue to inspire and educate, ensuring that their impact is felt for generations to come.

Aunt Marie's journey is intertwined with the history of the Apollo Theatre, the Harlem Renaissance, and the civil rights movement. Her life is a bridge between these iconic moments in history, connecting the past to the present and inspiring future generations. As we celebrate her 90th birthday and the 90th anniversary of the Apollo Theatre, we are reminded of the enduring power of art, culture, and activism to shape our world.

It is with deep gratitude and profound respect that I dedicate this book to Aunt Marie Scott Nance. Her life and legacy are a source of inspiration, and her unwavering commitment to justice and equity is a beacon of hope. This book is a testament to her influence, a celebration of her contributions, and a tribute to the enduring legacy of Ethel Ray Nance and the Harlem Renaissance.

Acknowledgment

This book is the result of years of research, storytelling, and a deep commitment to honoring the legacy of Ethel Ray Nance. I extend my deepest gratitude to those who have supported this work, including scholars, historians, family members, and community advocates who have shared their knowledge, memories, and resources.

This book would not have been possible without the preservation of Ethel's documents over the years. Ethel noted on several occasions that her father, William Henry Ray, encouraged her to write letters of her experiences, and he kept her letters, for which she was eternally grateful. When she passed in 1992, her son, Glenn Ray Nance, preserved his grandfather William Henry Ray's documents, along with his mother's invaluable records. When Uncle Glenn passed in 2022, his and Aunt Marie's eldest son, Craig T. Nance, carefully preserved these historical documents and graciously passed them on to me for safekeeping. It is only because of my family's dedication to preserving this amazing history that this book has come to fruition, and I am truly grateful.

I am especially appreciative of my great grandfather, William Henry Ray, my uncle, Glenn Ray Nance, my Aunt Marie Scott Nance, and my cousin, Craig T. Nance, whose dedication to preserving Ethel's legacy has been invaluable. Aunt Marie's insights, stories, and wisdom have provided a richer and more complete understanding of Ethel's impact. Additionally, I would like to thank the curators and archivists who have safeguarded the historical documents, photographs, and letters that shaped this narrative.

To all those who continue to celebrate and uplift the history of the Harlem Renaissance, I offer my deepest gratitude. Your work ensures that the voices of trailblazers like Ethel Ray Nance will never be forgotten.

Table of Contents

Dedication iii

Acknowledgment viii

Table of Contents x

Foreword xiii

About the Author xv

Preface: A Seat at the Table xvii

Introduction: Setting the Table xxiii

Part I: Foundations of Resilience 1

Chapter 1: Roots of Strength 2

Chapter 2: Opportunity Through Fire 9

Chapter 3. A Transformative Journey 11

Chapter 4: A Community Shattered, A Movement Born 19

Part II. Breaking Barriers and Expanding Horizons 24

Chapter 5. The Minnesota Legislature 25

Chapter 6. When the World Came to Kansas City: The Birthplace of the Harlem Renaissance 34

Part III: A Journey to Harlem 46

Chapter 7. Harlem Bound: Arriving in the Heart of a Movement 47

Chapter 8. The Diabolical Ray: Ethel's Ties to Harlem's Luminaries 55

Chapter 9: Dream Haven: A Cultural Oasis in Harlem . 59

Part IV: The Renaissance Unfolds 65

Chapter 10: The Opportunity Dinner 66

Chapter 11: A Night at Dream Haven 73

The Gang's All Here 76

Their Contributions to the Harlem Renaissance 77

Preservation of the Photographs 80

Chapter 12: Luminaries and Legacy: Shaping the Harlem Renaissance 82

Eric Walrond: Bringing the Caribbean and Harlem 130

Claude Barnett and Aaron Douglas: They called her "Jimmie" ~ The Visionary & the Artist. 136

Shared Legacies: The Philosopher, the Labor Leader & Activist, and the Historian & Poet Alain Locke: The Philosopher of the Renaissance 145

A. Philip Randolph: The Labor Leader and Activist 146

Arna Bontemps: Chronicling History Through Poetry 148

Shared Legacies: Locke, Randolph, and Bontemps 149

Countee Cullen: The Poet's Elegance 150

Langston Hughes: The Rhythm and Voice of a Movement 157

xi

Countie Cullen and Langston Hughes: Poets of the Renaissance..*164*

The Bonds That Shaped a Movement: Ethel Ray Nance & Harlem's Giants..*164*

Chapter 13: A Voice That Lifted a Nation: James Weldon Johnson's Enduring Legacy 166

Chapter 14: Fact or Fiction..170

Myths and Realities of Ethel Ray Nance and Regina Anderson Andrews...*170*

Speculative Narratives *173*

Chapter 15: "It Felt Like the End of Life": Returning to Duluth..175

Sustaining the Spirit of Harlem...*181*

The Apollo Theatre: A Legacy of Performance and Power *184*

The Edge Harlem: A Living Tribute.................................*185*

Part V: A Legacy That Lives On 187

Chapter 16. The Power of Symbolism and Legacy 188

Chapter 17: A Call to Action for Future Generations ..189

Epilogue..190

About the Author 193

Foreword

The Harlem Renaissance was one of the most transformative cultural movements in American history. It was a time when Black artists, intellectuals, and activists reshaped the national dialogue, creating works that illuminated the struggles, triumphs, and creativity of Black life. Despite the prominent figures often recognized, there were many whose contributions, though vital, have not received the same attention. Ethel Ray Nance is one such figure, a woman whose life and work exemplify resilience, intellect, and dedication to justice.

As a pioneering stenographer, the first Black female police officer in Minnesota, and an essential figure in organizations like the National Urban League and the NAACP, Ethel Ray Nance left an indelible mark on history. Yet, her role in the Harlem Renaissance remains largely unsung. Her story, interwoven with the luminaries of the time, deserves recognition and celebration.

In 2024 and 2025, several significant anniversaries converge, highlighting Ethel's remarkable journey and the broader cultural movements she influenced. This period marks the 125th anniversary of Ethel Ray Nance's birth in 1899, the 100th anniversary of her arrival in Harlem in 1925, and the 100th anniversary of the Opportunity Dinner, which served as a catalyst for the Harlem Renaissance. Additionally, 2024 marks the 90th anniversary of the Apollo Theatre, an enduring symbol of Black artistic excellence, and the 10th anniversary of The Edge Harlem restaurant, a venue housed in the same building where Ethel, Regina Anderson, and Louella Tucker once lived—a space historically known as Dream Haven. These anniversaries remind us of the deep connections between past and present and the spaces that continue to honor the legacies of those who shaped history.

This book not only recounts Ethel's journey but also serves as a reminder of the many individuals who shaped history from the sidelines—people whose impact was no less profound simply because they were not always at the forefront. Ethel's experiences, preserved through letters and historical documents, paint a vivid picture of her life's work and the movement she helped build.

By documenting her legacy, this book contributes to the broader mission of ensuring that every individual who shaped the Harlem Renaissance and the larger fight for racial justice is remembered. As you turn these pages, you will come to appreciate Ethel Ray Nance's critical role in shaping the narrative of Black excellence, resilience, and cultural empowerment.

About the Author

Karen Felecia Nance is an author, attorney, mediator, private investigator, and advocate whose work centers on justice, equality, and historical preservation. Through her writing, she sheds light on the extraordinary contributions of Ethel Ray Nance and other trailblazers who have shaped the fight for civil rights and social progress.

Karen has published the following works:

1. *My Father Poisoned Me, Or Did He?*
   A compelling memoir that delves into family, identity, and truth-seeking, exploring personal and historical narratives with depth and introspection.
2. *Ethel Ray Nance: Living in the White, Gray, and Black*
   A powerful biography that chronicles Ethel Ray Nance's groundbreaking work in civil rights, law enforcement, and racial inequities. This book highlights Nance's role in documenting Black history and fostering cross-cultural understanding.
3. *From Ethel Ray Nance to Kamala Harris: A Legacy of Equality and Justice*
   This work bridges historical and contemporary struggles for racial and gender equality, drawing a line from Ethel Ray Nance's activism to the rise of Kamala Harris, the first woman and first Black and South Asian Vice President of the United States.

Through her writing, Karen Felecia Nance preserves and amplifies the legacy of Ethel Ray Nance, ensuring that her impact on civil rights, literature, and social justice remains recognized and celebrated. These books represent only a sliver of the rich history she is committed to uncovering, with much more to come.

Karen continues to advocate for historical truth, intersectional justice, and community empowerment, using her platform to connect past struggles with present-day activism.

Preface: A Seat at the Table

The Harlem Renaissance stands as one of the most vibrant and transformative cultural movements in American history, a time when Black artists, intellectuals, and activists gave voice to a collective experience of resilience, beauty, and defiance in the face of systemic racism. Amid the luminaries of this era, the contributions of figures like Ethel Ray Nance are often overshadowed despite their undeniable importance. This book, *A Seat at the Table: Ethel Ray Nance and the Harlem Renaissance*, aims to restore her rightful place in the historical record, shedding light on her remarkable legacy and her enduring impact on the Harlem Renaissance and beyond.

Carl Van Vechten played a pivotal role in bringing greater visibility to the Harlem Renaissance, using his influence as a writer and photographer to champion Black art, music, and literature to mainstream audiences. Yet, his involvement remains deeply controversial. Van Vechten was often criticized for his portrayal of Black culture, particularly in his early writings, where he perpetuated troubling stereotypes, claiming that Black people were naturally suited to be entertainers and sexually "free." Many contemporaries and later critics viewed him as an outsider, a white man profiting from and interpreting a culture that was not his own. This duality of Van Vechten's role as promoter and cultural gatekeeper, yet also a source of division, has sparked ongoing debates about cultural appropriation, allyship, and representation.

Amid these complex dynamics, Ethel Ray Nance stood as a critical figure who navigated multiple worlds with grace and purpose. More than a participant, she was a pioneer who forged paths where none had existed before. Her involvement in civil rights work, her role as a groundbreaking stenographer, and her ability to advocate for justice through both her words and actions exemplify her quiet yet profound influence. Unlike Van Vechten, Nance did not stand on the periphery observing cultural movements; she lived it, shaped it, and carried its torch forward in ways that are often overlooked.

This sentiment is poignantly captured in a letter dated May 28, 1985, from Professor Bruce Kellner of Millersville University, author of *Carl Van Vechten and the Irreverent Decades.* In this letter, Kellner acknowledges Nance's invaluable contributions and recounts a conversation with her son, Glenn. Kellner shares that he urged Glenn to "sit [her] down with a tape recorder one of these days and get [her] to recall EVERYTHING." He continues, "Certainly, you gave ample evidence of a nearly flawless memory, and your role in the Harlem Renaissance is far more valuable than you probably realize."

MILLERSVILLE UNIVERSITY

Millersville University of Pennsylvania
Millersville, Pennsylvania 17551

28 May 1985

My dear Mrs Nance,

I don't know whether or not you care to have a copy of this paper about Carl Van Vechten. I know you had said you might have to leave before I read it, but you can imagine my enormous pride and pleasure in seeing you in the audience.

As for that, I hope you realize the pride and pleasure that MANY people felt in having your at the conference, and I am in your permanent debt for having agreed to join that panel. For me, you were the real star of the show! (Bruce Nugent, who is usually loquacious on such occasions, was curiously quiet, but I think he was very tired at that point in the proceedings; Mrs Cullen and Mrs Woodruff, of course, were not really on the scene at the time; and Miss Burke was only just beginning. You, on the other hard, were our living history for the day!) And what you had to say was exactly right for the occasion.

I told Glenn -- to whom I send my very best wishes -- that I hoped he'd sit you down with a tape recorder one of these days and get you to recall EVERYTHING. Certainly, you gave ample evidence of a nearly flawless memory, and your role in the Harlem Renaissance is far more valuable than you probably realize.

Thank you again for bringing the conference to life for so many people.

Sincerely, Bruce Kellner

Letter from Bruce Kellner to Mrs. (Ethel) Nance dated May 28, 1985

Though Glenn Ray Nance did not have the opportunity to sit with his mother and capture all of her memories in her own voice, Ethel left behind jewels in the form of photographs, postcards, letters, and other valuable materials. These cherished items, filled with personal reflections and historical insights, have shaped the heart of this book. They stand as tangible echoes of Ethel's life and legacy, treasures that bridge the past to the present and provide a rich tapestry of her remarkable journey.

It has been a century since Ethel Ray Nance arrived in Harlem in 1924, marking the beginning of her extraordinary contributions to a cultural movement that redefined the identity of Black America. As we celebrate 125 years since her birth, we also commemorate key milestones that highlight the enduring legacy of the Harlem Renaissance. On March 21, 2025, Opportunity Dinner celebrated its 100th anniversary, a pivotal event that launched the Harlem Renaissance and catalyzed a period of unparalleled artistic and intellectual achievement.

This historic era gave rise to icons who transformed literature, music, and art, with Harlem as its epicenter. The 90th anniversary of the Apollo Theater in 2024 stands as a testament to the movement's impact. Since 1934, the Apollo has been a center of Black cultural excellence, highlighting legendary talents and inspiring creativity across generations. Additionally, 2024 marks the 10th anniversary of The Edge Harlem, a restaurant located at the very site where Ethel Ray Nance, Regina Anderson Andrews, and Louella Tucker once shared a home. This space served as a gathering place for some of the greatest minds of the Harlem

Renaissance and now carries forward their legacy by blending Harlem's rich history with contemporary culture.

Together, these milestones reflect a legacy of resilience, innovation, and cultural pride that continues to shape our understanding of history and inspire future generations. This convergence of anniversaries serves as a powerful reminder of how history, legacy, and culture remain interconnected across time and space. They not only honor the past but also invite reflection on how far we have come and how much further we must go to achieve true justice and equity.

This book exists to ensure that Ethel Ray Nance's voice and contributions are not lost to history. Her story challenges the traditional narratives that often center on male leaders or white allies, offering instead a nuanced portrayal of a Black woman whose work bridged cultural, racial, and geographical boundaries. By amplifying Nance's legacy, this book seeks to honor not only her memory but also the countless women and unsung heroes whose efforts laid the foundation for progress.

As readers journey through these pages, they will encounter not only the triumphs and trials of Ethel Ray Nance but also the broader context of a world grappling with profound social change. Her story invites us to consider what it means to live authentically, to persevere in the face of adversity, and to contribute meaningfully to a legacy larger than oneself. In doing so, it provides a lens through which we can better understand our shared history and, perhaps, find inspiration for the work that remains in our present and future.

A Seat at the Table is a celebration, a reclamation, and a reminder of the enduring power of one woman's contributions to the Harlem Renaissance, a movement that, at its core, called for justice, dignity, and the recognition of the humanity and creativity of Black Americans. It is also a testament to the importance of preserving these stories, as Professor Kellner so eloquently reminded us in his letter to Ethel. By doing so, we honor the past and chart the course toward a more inclusive and truthful historical narrative.

Introduction: Setting the Table

In 2024, four extraordinary events converge: the 125th birthday of Ethel Ray Nance, the 100th anniversary of Ethel's arrival in Harlem, the 90th anniversary of the Apollo Theatre, and the 10th anniversary of The Edge Harlem restaurant. In 2025, we celebrate the 100th anniversary of the Harlem Renaissance. Together, these milestones weave a tapestry of resilience, creativity, and cultural pride, celebrating the transformative power of individuals, movements, and spaces that honor the past while inspiring the future.

The 125th anniversary of Ethel Ray Nance's birth is a moment to reflect on the extraordinary life of a woman whose legacy exemplifies courage, perseverance, and innovation. Born in Duluth, Minnesota, in 1899, Ethel was a trailblazer who broke barriers as a stenographer, police officer, and cultural advocate. Her work spanned generations and geographies, from Minnesota's fight for racial equality to Harlem's creative renaissance. Ethel's contributions to the National Urban League, the NAACP, and the Harlem Renaissance made her a vital force in the fight for racial justice and the celebration of Black identity. Her 125th birthday reminds us of the timeless relevance of her story and the strength of her vision, a story that this book seeks to honor under the title, *A Seat at the Table: Ethel Ray Nance and the Harlem Renaissance.*

The 100th anniversary of the Harlem Renaissance in 2025 underscores the profound impact of a cultural awakening that redefined Black identity and creativity. This transformative movement gave rise to groundbreaking art, literature, and activism, with Harlem at its epicenter. Ethel Ray Nance, deeply engaged in the movement, collaborated with luminaries like W.E.B. Du Bois, creating a legacy of intellectual and artistic excellence. The Harlem Renaissance's centennial invites reflection on how its spirit continues to shape modern cultural and social landscapes.

The 90th anniversary of the Apollo Theatre celebrates an iconic institution that has stood as a beacon of Black artistry since its opening in 1934. The Apollo provided a stage for legends like Billie Holiday, Ella Fitzgerald, James Brown, and Aretha Franklin, solidifying Harlem's reputation as a cultural capital. The Apollo remains a vital space for fostering talent and celebrating the contributions of Black artists, ensuring that its 90-year legacy endures for generations to come.

The 10th anniversary of The Edge Harlem restaurant highlights the intersection of Harlem's historic and contemporary spirit. Located at the former home of Ethel Ray Nance and her roommates Regina Andrews and Luella Tucker, The Edge serves as a culinary and cultural hub. By blending international flavors with Harlem's rich heritage, the restaurant honors the neighborhood's history while providing a modern space for dialogue, creativity, and community. Its anniversary is a testament to Harlem's resilience and its ongoing role as a center of innovation and legacy.

This book takes readers on a journey through Ethel's life, the Renaissance she helped shape, the Apollo's lasting impact, and the present-day celebrations of Harlem's enduring spirit. It is a tribute to the synergy of these anniversaries and a call to action for future generations to continue building on the foundations of resilience, creativity, and cultural pride.

Throughout this journey, Ethel's own words serve as a guiding voice. As a meticulous record-keeper, she documented her experiences, thoughts, and reflections in her personal diary, offering rare insight into the struggles and triumphs she witnessed firsthand. These diary excerpts, preserved within the Nance family's private collection, provide an intimate connection to her perspective and the history she helped shape. Where appropriate, they are included in this book with minimal edits for clarity, ensuring that her voice remains at the forefront of her story. Rather than being footnoted separately, these excerpts are seamlessly woven into the narrative, allowing readers to experience Ethel's world as she saw it.

Her words remind us that history is not merely a collection of events but the lived experiences of those who dared to challenge injustice and dream of a better future. By sharing her diary alongside historical accounts, this book honors her legacy and invites readers to walk alongside her, seeing the world through her eyes and drawing inspiration from her journey.

Plans are underway to preserve the diary in a historical archive for future research.

Part I:
Foundations of Resilience

Karen Felecia Nance

Chapter 1:
Roots of Strength

Ethel Ray Nance's upbringing in Duluth laid the foundation for her resilience, ambition, and unshakable commitment to justice, traits that would later echo in the cultural movements and institutions she influenced. Born on April 13, 1899, to William Henry Ray, a Black laborer and activist from North Carolina, and Inga Nordquist, a Swedish immigrant, Ethel grew up in a household shaped by both love and profound challenges. Her parents' unique partnership blended their distinct cultural identities, creating an environment that celebrated resilience, determination, and a belief in the transformative power of education and activism.

William Henry Ray & Inga Nordquist Ray 1889, private collection of Karen Felecia Nance

A Seat at the Table: Ethel Ray Nance & the Harlem Renaissance

In 1900, tragedy struck when Ethel's eldest sister, Ora, died of pneumonia at just seven years old.

William & Inga's oldest two children: William Nordquist & Ora Inga Ray abt 1895, Two Harbors, Minnesota, private collection of Karen Felecia Nance.

The loss devastated her parents, Inga, a devoted and nurturing mother, and William Henry, a stoic yet deeply grieving father, and left a void that profoundly affected the family dynamics. With Ora gone, Ethel became her parents' only daughter and the glue that held the family together.

William Nordquist Ray, Inga Nordquist Ray & Oscar Edwin Ray at Ora Inga Ray's Funeral, 1900, private collection of Karen Felecia Nance

Ethel May Ray, 1900, private collection of Karen Felecia Nance

While they had two sons, Will and Oscar, it was Ethel who seemed to embody the emotional core of the household. Her mother often leaned on Ethel for companionship, while her father saw in her a reflection of his own strength and determination.

The family's unwavering love for Ethel was laced with an unspoken fear of losing her, a fear that shaped their protectiveness and fueled her own drive to succeed. Despite systemic racism and financial barriers, Ethel excelled academically. She demonstrated natural charisma and leadership ability that set her apart. However, her aspirations to attend college were curtailed by the family's limited finances and societal prejudices that excluded young Black women from many opportunities. Ethel's determination to overcome these barriers would shape her life and legacy.

Duluth's small Black community, comprising only about 200 people in a city of nearly 100,000 in 1920, was both a source of solidarity and a stark reminder of their minority status. Her father, William Henry, instilled in Ethel and her brothers the importance of education, pride, and integrity, urging them to maintain self-respect in a world that often denied them basic rights. Inga, though loving and supportive, could not shield her children from the racial prejudice that permeated their lives.

Ethel and her two older brothers, Will and Oscar, attended both St. Paul's Episcopal Church, a predominantly white congregation, and St. Mark's AME Church, which served a mainly Black community. The progressive minister of St. Paul's, Dr. Albert Ryan, welcomed the Ray children and created an environment where Ethel could cultivate her leadership skills. She became a trusted helper in the church and eventually served as president of the Philathea Class, a group for young people. However, not all parishioners shared Dr. Ryan's inclusive perspective. Ethel was the Sunday school teacher of a class where one of her students developed a very close bond with where and often brought her small gifts. When the child's mother discovered that Ethel was Black, she withdrew her daughter from the class after Reverend Ryan refused to remove Ethel as the teacher at the mother's request. It remained a particularly painful memory for Ethel, who had cherished the connection she shared with the child. This rejection left a lasting impression on Ethel, reinforcing her determination to combat societal prejudices.

Upon graduating from high school in 1918, Ethel Ray Nance took several federal civil service examinations, passed them successfully, and received forms from Washington asking routine questions about her willingness to accept employment in local, Washington-based, or other territorial jobs. She consistently responded "yes" to all inquiries. Despite this, no appointments followed. Frustrated, she enlisted the help of Reverend Ryan of St. Paul's to contact Congressman Clarence B. Miller of the 8th District on her behalf. *Miller's reply on the following page.* Ethel was disheartened to read: "The color line will interfere in these appointments since most of the officials are now southern Democrats, and you know how they feel about our colored people."

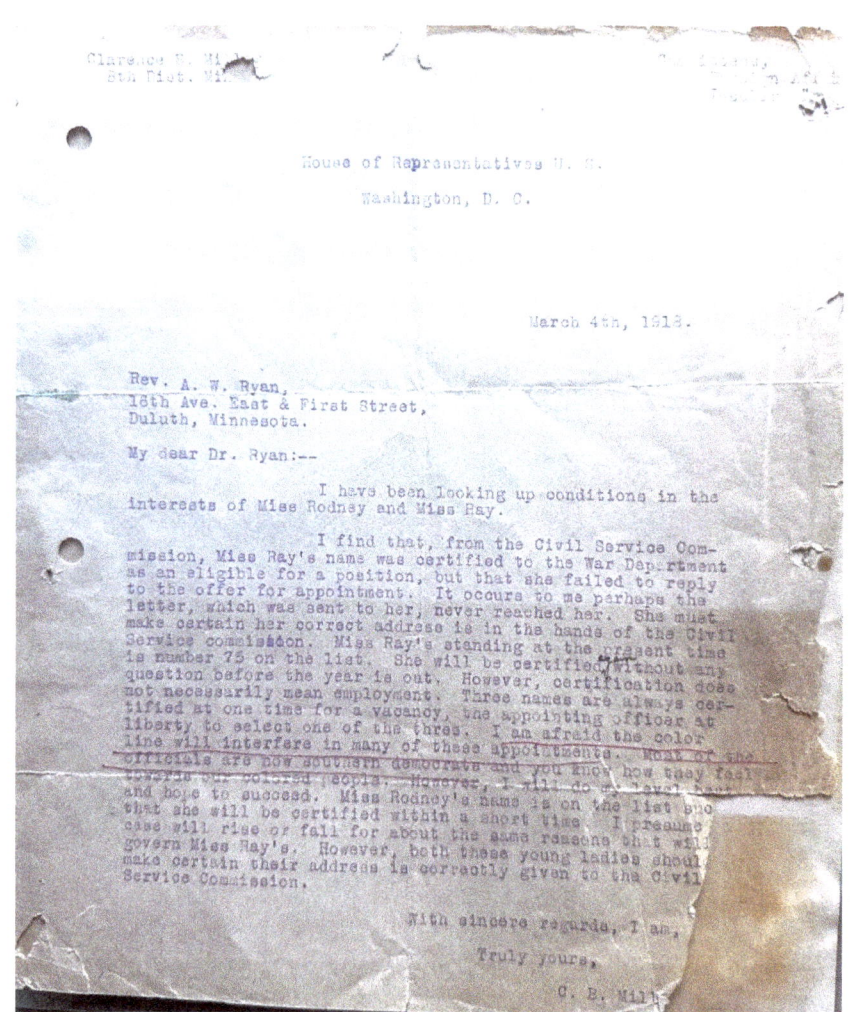

Letter from Congressman C.B. Miller to Rev. A.W. Ryan dated March 4, 1918

Chapter 2: Opportunity Through Fire

In October 1918, tragedy struck northern Minnesota when a series of devastating wildfires swept through the Cloquet, Moose Lake, and Duluth areas. The fires left over 500 people dead and caused $30 million in property damage, displacing thousands.

The Governor of Minnesota appointed a Forest Fire Relief Commission in collaboration with the American Red Cross to assist survivors. Colonel H.V. Eva, the State Director, called for volunteers, and Ethel eagerly applied. Having worked with Colonel Eva during the Liberty Loan Drive, Ethel's qualifications secured her position as an interviewer of refugees and stenographer at the emergency relief headquarters in Duluth.

After two months in Duluth, Ethel was transferred to Moose Lake, the community most severely affected by the fires. Moose Lake presented stark challenges for Ethel. The rural town harbored overt racial hostility, and Black train workers who traveled between Duluth and the Twin Cities had long shared stories of being harassed by locals.

Ethel's father had warned her about Moose Lake's prejudice, but she was still unprepared for the blatant hostility she encountered. Despite her professional demeanor and essential role in relief efforts, Ethel faced animosity from residents who viewed her with suspicion and disdain. Her experience in Moose Lake was a painful reminder of the systemic barriers she would face throughout her life.

Ethel's work involved interviewing displaced families, documenting their losses, and coordinating aid distribution. The long hours, emotional toll, and racial hostility tested her resolve, but she remained steadfast in her commitment to helping those in need. This period of her life strengthened her resilience and fueled her determination to fight for justice and equality.

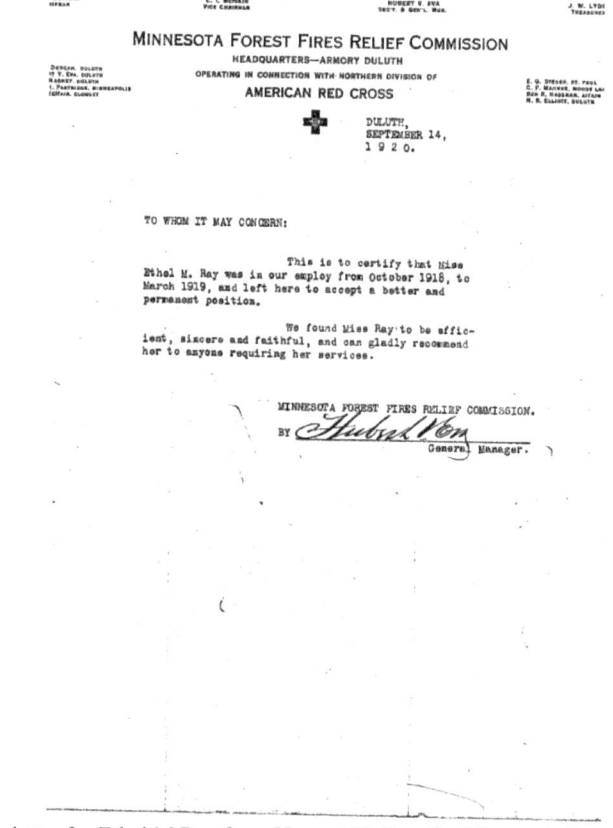

Reference letter for Ethel M Ray from Hervert V. Eva, the Minnesota Forest Fires Relief Commission: To Whom It May Concern. Dated September 14, 1920

Chapter 3. A Transformative Journey

In 1919, the population of Duluth was about 100,000 residents with only about 200 of which were Black. Despite the limited social opportunities for young Black people in the city, Ethel would return home from Moose Lake for holidays and other occasions to spend time with family. However, summer in Duluth brought a glimpse of diversity when passenger boats arrived carrying Black college students from Howard, Fisk, and other Historically Black Colleges and Universities. These students worked seasonal jobs to help fund their tuition, and their presence enlivened the community.

Ethel treasured these summers, which included afternoon matinee dances arranged by mothers who ensured proper chaperons were present to observe the young men with their daughters. These gatherings provided social connection and inspiration, exposing Ethel to the world of higher education and reinforcing her own aspirations for academic and professional development beyond Duluth.

Ethel's father, William Henry Ray, was wary of these visiting college students. He understood Ethel's yearning for a broader world and worried that their charming stories of academic life might further motivate her to leave Duluth for prestigious Black colleges. Perhaps in response to this, he planned a transformative father-daughter trip to the East and South, offering her a broader perspective while keeping her under his guidance.

When William Henry Ray initially told Ethel they were heading directly to Raleigh, North Carolina, to see property that belonged to his father, Henry Ray, so she would be able to identify it in the future. However, when they departed, they first traveled to Chicago, where Ethel saw the Negro YMCA and the Urban League for the first time. It was only then that she realized that her father had a carefully arranged itinerary with stops he had not disclosed to her.

They arrived in Chicago shortly after race riots had ravaged the city. This was Ethel's first real glimpse of a bustling metropolis with towering buildings and crowded streets. The palpable racial tension and firsthand accounts of violence left a deep impression on her. She and her father heard firsthand testimony about the riots, a harrowing experience that shaped her understanding of racial injustice. At the YMCA on 38th and Wabasha, they met Frayer T. Lane, the Executive Secretary of the Community Service Urban League in Chicago. At this stop, and at every stop after, Ethel would always ask if there was an opening for a stenographer, and almost always there was.

Little did Ethel know that three years later, she would find herself working for F.T. Lane in Kansas City, Missouri, with the Urban League as office manager and head of the Girls and Women's Department.

From Chicago, they traveled to Ohio, stopping in Cincinnati at the Ohio River. Her father explained its historical significance, noting that this was the same river mentioned in Harriet Beecher Stowe's *Uncle Tom's Cabin*, where Eliza crossed the ice with her child, fleeing the slave catchers. This journey, thrilling yet deeply educational, continuously emphasized the importance of Black history and the ongoing fight for justice. Though Ethel sometimes found her father's lessons exhausting, Ethel later recognized how much they shaped her perspective.

In Philadelphia, they visited landmarks such as the Crispus Attucks monument, Faneuil Hall, and Prince Hall's gravesite, honoring the founder of the Colored Masonic Lodge, of which her father was a member. A particularly notable moment was meeting Monroe Trotter, editor of *The Guardian,* a publication her father deeply admired.

William Henry Ray & Ethel May Ray at Crispus Attucks Statute, Boston, Massachusetts, 1920, private collection of Karen Felecia Nance.

Their travels took them from Boston to New York City, where they visited the NAACP (National Association for the Advancement of Colored People) office. William Henry Ray had hoped to meet Dr. W.E.B. Du Bois, the director of research and the editor of *The Crisis*, the official magazine of the NAACP, but was disappointed to learn that he was in Europe attending the Pan-African Conference. However, they met other influential figures, including William Pickens. They explored Harlem and stopped by the

Messenger office to meet A. Philip Randolph and George Schuyler, and toured the Harlem Library and other significant sites that would later shape Ethel's life. Reflecting on this whirlwind visit, she wrote in her diary, "New York was just too much of everything—people, places, hustle and bustle."

Next, they traveled to Washington, D.C., where Ethel reconnected with two girls from Duluth and visited Howard University. During the visit, her father cautioned her about young men who had spent summers in Duluth, claiming to attend Howard, suggesting that their connection to the university might be as tenuous as her own experience walking its halls.

After spending two months in the South, they returned to the Midwest, stopping by the NAACP office in New York City, where William Henry Ray finally met Dr. Du Bois. William shared with him that his father had property in Raleigh, North Carolina, and expressed a desire for Ethel to understand the stark differences in life for Blacks in the North and the South. He also wanted her to contribute to the betterment of the Black race. During their visit to North Carolina, a relative who taught in a one-room school fell ill, and Ethel stepped in to teach for two weeks. The school, situated about a mile through the woods, housed roughly 50 pupils, with an average attendance of 20 to 25, ranging in age from 7 to 19. This seemed the role William envisioned for Ethel, helping to educate the next generation in the South.

Ethel wasn't certain if Dr. Du Bois sensed her reluctance, but he shared his own experiences teaching in the South, cautioning about the limited impact one could have in such isolated environments. He suggested that working with organizations in larger cities would be a more effective way to challenge systemic injustice. Because of William Henry Rays's deep respect for Dr. Du Bois, Ethel was never again pressured into working in rural Southern schools. Ethel often remarked that her father revered Dr. Du Bois: "There was God, and then there was Dr. Du Bois."

The vibrancy of Harlem thrilled Ethel but also overwhelmed her. When she returned to Duluth, she carried a profound sense of awe and a yearning for a future beyond her hometown. This journey opened her eyes to the intellectual and activist circles, planting the seeds of her future work. When they arrived back home, her father told her mother, "I brought her back, but I wasn't sure I would be able to."

Throughout their travels, Ethel and her father often encountered people curious about life in the North. William Henry Ray enthusiastically shared his perspective, emphasizing the opportunities for education and employment available to young Black people. He reassured many, saying, "You have an opportunity for schooling, you can get work, and while the white people don't exactly love you, the important thing is that the law will protect you."

Tragically, this optimism was shattered after their return to Minnesota. On June 15, 1920, three Black circus workers, Elmer Jackson, Elias Clayton, and Isaac McGhie, were lynched in Duluth after being falsely accused of assaulting a white woman. A mob of 5,000 people seized the men from the jail and lynched them in a public square just four blocks from Ethel's home. At the time, Ethel was in Moose Lake, assisting with the Minnesota Forest Fire Relief efforts. When news of the lynching reached her, she felt a palpable hostility in the town's atmosphere, as if many locals approved of the atrocity.

This horrifying event was a turning point in her life, solidifying her resolve to fight racial injustice. The lynching shattered the illusion of safety for Duluth's small Black community. Southern newspapers cruelly headlined the event as a lynching in the "Free North," underscoring the painful reality that racism knew no geographic bounds.

# The Duluth Lynching
What Press Says of Hanging Three Negroes

An editorial in the Chicago Tribune says:

Duluth has now joined the American cities which have discovered how easily the safeguards of civilized justice can be leaped. Suddenness is a common factor of all such outbreaks and law finally reasserts itself, but after lives are sacrificed and the community's good name is besmirched.

In Omaha, it was said, delays and failure of justice in cases of offenses against women had inflamed public feeling. Pictures of the mob showed callousness and irresponsibility rather than uncontrollable passion. The delay of justic theory did not bear examination very well. In the Duluth lynching it seems to have less validity if it has any.

The problem is deeper. At its base, of course, is a very strong trait in American character which creates, in spite of inconsistencies and exceptions, a special attitude toward women. In the Duluth case the men charged with the offense were negroes, and undoubtedly this was an important factor in the psychology of the outbreak. But white men are sometimes lynched for this offense when circumstances are aggravated. In the Duluth lynching motives of sex protection and of race instinct were combined.

We can eradicate neither and we would eradicate neither. Both are useful, perhaps necessary if properly controlled and directed. But they were not controlled in Duluth, as they were not controlled in Chicago, in Omaha, in Springfield. The authorities of Duluth permitted the leaders of the mob to go about in automobiles gathering recruits for the lynching. This was a sign of inefficiency, of lax police discipline, if not of connivance, which challenges the self-respect of Duluth and warns the responsible elements of its population that the morale of its police protection is low. Prompt arrest of the mob leaders would have saved a blot on the city's schutcheon and perhaps the lives of innocent men.

That is for Duluth to think about; but all America has in this new lynching a cause for the gravest reflection. The Duluth mob herd appeals to let the law take its course. Its members did not heed these appeals because they themselves wanted to kill. We doubt if they were certain as to the guilt of the men who died asserting their innocence; but they wanted victims to assuage their lust for vengeance, and victims they would have, whether innocent or guilty. We doubt if the uncertainty and tardiness of legal processes of justice have much to do with lynch phychology, but we think it might be tempered by a keener sense of responsibility to the law. Mobs, and even mob leaders, are seldom punished. Until they are there is little to check the lynching evil.

We hope Duluth will do better than other cities in dealing with the men who have brought stain to her good name. Duluth is a very proud city and may set us all an example. We certainly need one. Mob violence is inexcusable in civilized communities. The American lynching is a disgrace to us the world over.

* * *

The Superior Telegram in part says:

"Duluth has a serious problem on its hands as an aftermath to the triple lynching that occurred in that city Tuesday night. An investigation of the failure of the police to cope with the riot situation is under way and a grand jury has been summoned for the purpose of bringing to justice those guilty of participation in the mob's crime.

"The entire country will watch the outcome of the investigation of the handling of the affair by the police. Duluth's standing as a law-loving and law-abiding city will depend much on the verdict and sequel to this investigation, for it will disclose either a lamentably weak and inefficient leadership or else a policy so treacherous and alarming as to demand heroic measures lest it lead toward veritable chaos.

"The question now at issue is whether the police of Duluth did their duty in attempting to prevent the commission of another crime by a mob of citizens who had been worked into a frenzy. The orders obeyed by the Duluth police were that no blood be shed. No firearms were to be used."

The Duluth News Tribune, Duluth, MN, Saturday, June 19, 1920.

Chapter 4: A Community Shattered, A Movement Born

William Henry Ray had long held a vision of the North as a beacon of hope, a land where opportunities flourished, and justice was within reach, especially for marginalized communities. This belief sustained him through years of struggle and aspiration.

However, on June 15, 1920, that belief was irrevocably shattered. The lynching of three Black men in Duluth, mere blocks from the Ray family home, served as a brutal reminder that the scourge of white supremacy was not confined to the South. This horrific act of racial violence revealed the pervasive nature of racism, even in places that were thought to be more progressive.

For William Henry Ray, this event was a moment of profound disillusionment. The ideals he had cherished were laid bare, exposing the stark contrast between hope and reality. Ethel, too, felt the weight of this tragedy deeply. It was not just a loss of faith in a better future but a devastating blow to the very fabric of their community. The incident marked a turning point for the Ray family, forcing them to confront the unsettling truth that justice was still a distant dream, fraught with peril and inequity.

Until that night, she had been a young woman shaped by the cultural richness of her mixed heritage. Her mother, Inga Nordquist, carried the traditions of her Swedish homeland, where resilience and close-knit community bonds were paramount. Her father, William

Henry Ray, was the son of enslaved people who had fought for their freedom and for the generations to come. From him, she learned the weight of history and the responsibility to act. The contrast of privilege and oppression within her own lineage sharpened her awareness, preparing her for the battle ahead.

Her father's reaction to the lynchings was swift and resolute. William Henry Ray stepped forward to establish Duluth's chapter of the NAACP, ensuring that the community's grief was transformed into action. At his side, Ethel witnessed the power of organizing—collecting signatures for the Dyer Anti-Lynching Bill, gathering people for meetings, and writing letters to lawmakers. It was no longer enough to simply hope for change; she had to help create it.

The fear that gripped Duluth's Black residents was suffocating. If such horror could unfold in their own neighborhood, what safety did they truly have? Yet, in their fear, there was also determination. Ethel, emboldened by the moment, took a decisive step. At her father's urging, she reached out to Dr. W.E.B. Du Bois, the nation's leading Black intellectual and co-founder of the NAACP, to come to Duluth and speak. When Dr. Du Bois agreed, Ethel personally accompanied him on the train from St. Paul to Duluth—a journey that marked the beginning of a lifelong mentorship.

On March 21, 1921, before a packed audience at St. Mark's AME Church, Ethel introduced Dr. Du Bois. He spoke with precision and passion, urging the Black community to stand firm in the face of injustice, to organize, and to demand their rights. His words electrified the room, giving voice to the unspoken fears and unyielding hopes of those who had gathered. For Ethel, the moment was transformative. It was no longer just about reacting to injustice; it was about becoming part of the movement that could dismantle it.

Dr. Du Bois's visit elevated the work of Duluth's NAACP chapter, but it also cemented his connection to the Ray family. Whenever he returned to Minnesota, he made their home his own. Despite his reputation as a stern and uncompromising intellectual, Ethel saw another side of him—one that was patient with her mother, who struggled with English, and one that relished the warmth of family. He often teased Ethel about her coffee-brewing skills, turning even the simplest moments into lessons in persistence.

In the years that followed, Dr. Du Bois twice offered Ethel a position as his stenographer in New York, a rare opportunity for a Black woman at the time. But life at home intervened—her mother's health had declined, and Ethel could not leave. By the time she was free to go in 1924, the offer was no longer available. Instead, she took a position working for Dr. Charles S. Johnson, editor of *Opportunity* magazine. It was a choice that would place her at the center of one of the most vibrant cultural movements in history.

Exactly four years after Du Bois's speech in Duluth, on March 21, 1925, he attended the legendary Opportunity Dinner at the Civic Club in New York—a gathering of artists, writers, and intellectuals that ignited the Harlem Renaissance. As Johnson's assistant, Ethel played a key role in organizing the event. That night, the room buzzed with the voices of Langston Hughes, Zora Neale Hurston, and other rising luminaries. The energy was electric, a sign that a new Black artistic and intellectual movement was taking form.

Ethel had stepped beyond the borders of Duluth into a broader world of activism and cultural change. But the lessons of her father's work and the horrors of 1920 remained with her. The struggle for justice was far from over, and she would continue to walk the path of those who came before her—determined to make sure that the past would never be forgotten.

A Seat at the Table: Ethel Ray Nance & the Harlem Renaissance

DOCTOR DUBOIS LECTURED TO AN APPRECIATIVE HOUSE

White and Colored Citizens Packed St. Mark's M. E. Church to Hear Scholarly and Instructive Address By Noted Colored Champion and Leader of the Negro Race.

A packed house greeted Dr. W. E. B. DuBois when he lectured to a mixed audience at St. Mark's Methodist church a week ago last Monday evening on conditions that obtain and problems that confront the colored and white races, both in the United States and other parts of the world.

In a most instructive and convincing way, the speaker outlined the effects of segregation of the colored people, whether in the majority or the minority. He took examples from the Zulus in South Africa, republican Liberia, the black centers in the larger cities, rural and sparsely settled localities in Florida and other southern states. He took examples from his own native New England and the newer states in the West, particularly Oklahoma. Dr. DuBois did not espouse social equality for the colored people, but he did contend that a reasonable personal contact was necessary for both races. When that contact is denied, abnormal conditions arise that are inimical to the best interests of one race or the other, or even both. He contended that no race or nation can live alone. In the United States, especially, both whites and blacks are fellow citizens and it is up to them to solve the great problems that are due to the existence of 12,000,000 colored people, one tenth of a total population of 120,000,000 souls.

Dr. DuBois is a man of striking appearance. His short, pointed, upturned moustaches and his neatly trimmed goatee might cause one to consider him a military man, another a poet, another a novelist, a second Dumas, perhaps, or even a specialist in some professional line. He speaks with a scholarly and cultured accent in perfect English. His face is one to attract attention in any place at any time.

After being given a short, poetic and charming introduction by Miss Ethel Ray, Dr. DuBois quietly took his position at the speaker's stand, clasped his hands across the top and began to talk in earnest, convincing and even thrilling conversational tones, rarely raising his voice and not once, during the entire address, did he use his hands in an oratorical gesture. It was a rare exhibition of moderation and self-control, yet one felt that there was almost no limit to the reserve power of the man.

Today, Dr. DuBois probably is the most eminent and effective champion of the colored people in America, if not all the world. He is credited with being the worthy successor of the late Booker T. Washington. He is the editor of "The Crisis," a high-grade and very influential magazine published in Boston for the benefit of the colored race. Loyalty to his people impresses one even more than does his apparent ability. He has had the advantage of wide travel and personal contact with the conditions he tells about. It is to be regretted that a larger, more accessible place for the lecture could not have been secured and that thousands of white citizens of Duluth did not hear it. It is stated that downtown halls were denied those who had the appearance of Dr. DuBois in charge.

Dr. DuBois at present is director of publications and research of the National Association for the Advancement of Colored People. He was one of the organizers of that association, the very first to take the initiative, and the cause of that association was presented to the audience by Sergt. Kelley after the lecturer ended his effort. Both white and colored people are eligible to membership and the fee is only $1.00 a year. Those who join and pay $2.50, also get "The Crisis" for a year. Those who subscribe $5 and $10 a year, get certain credits and material benefits.

Dr. DuBois hopes for a membership of millions. The colored people of Duluth will be expected to secure enough memberships among their own race to aggregate a certain sum. But it is desired and planned to greatly exceed that quota by making a drive among the white people of Duluth for memberships.

This drive will extend from April 24 to May 8. It will be in charge of the local colored people with W. H. Lay as colonel. Messrs. W. H. Dawson, George Hall, H. B. Newsome and J. Malone, of Duluth and Webster, of Superior, have been commissioned captains. Other officers, such as majors, captains and lieutenants, with permanent commissions, will be appointed as soon as they qualify. Miss Ethel Ray, with rank of first Lieuten it, will have charge of the "minute men."

It is probable, also, that local white members of the Duluth branch of the National Association for the Advancement of Colored People will aid in the drive.

It is probable, also, that local white members of the Duluth branch of the National Association for the Advancement of Colored People will aid in the drive.

The National Association for the Advancement of Colored People is considered the one organization striving to make America a true democracy. Its members contend that so long as one tenth of this nation's population is denied the rights guaranteed to all citizens under the constitution, America cannot be truly "The land of the free."

RACES DEPENDENT UPON EACH OTHER, SAYS DR. DU BOIS

"If true democracy began at home, foreign nations would not criticize our attempts to carry it to the ends of the globe," Dr. W. E. B. Du Bois declared in a talk last night at St. Mark's Methodist church. Dr. Du Bois is the founder of the National Association for the Advancement of Colored People, the editor of the Crisis magazine, and the recognized successor of Booker T. Washington. A large audience, many of the white race, heard him.

"The war has proved that the interests of all people are so intertwined no people can live alone," he declared. "Liberia is a failure because it is a state isolated from the rest of the world.

"It is in protest against the treatment received from superior groups that negroes and others segregate themselves in our great cities. Their way of living are not in accordance with American ideals."

The program included vocal solos by W. B. Richardson and Mrs. Minnie Adams, a prayer by Rev. William Majors, a violin solo by Henry Williams and an introductory talk by Miss Ethel Ray.

The National Association for the Advancement of Colored People includes representatives of all people who are pledged to gain an understanding of how to obtain better relations between all races. Dr. Du Bois, as its founder, has received honorary degrees from a number of universities and has been widely recognized.

DR. W. E. DuBOIS
(Editor of "The Crisis")
Will LECTURE at the A. M. E. CHURCH
5th Ave. East & 6th St. Duluth
Monday Evening, March 21, 1921, at Eight o'Clock

Tickets Fifty Cents Each

The Duluth Herald, March 22, 1921 & March 28, 1921; Articles: Race Dependent Upon Each Other Says Dr. Du Bois; Doctor DuBois Lectured to an Appreciative House; Fifty cent ticket for entry

Part II. Breaking Barriers and Expanding Horizons

Chapter 5. The Minnesota Legislature

Ethel's resolve had been strengthened in the wake of the lynchings and her work with the NAACP in Duluth, but the hostility in Moose Lake lingered. The town's residents, largely indifferent to the injustice that had unfolded, justified the violence rather than condemning it. The atmosphere weighed heavily on her, intensifying her restlessness and pushing her to seek new opportunities.

A visit to St. Paul provided a much-needed change of scenery. Ethel stayed with family friend Ida Mae Murphy, and during her time there, Ida's father, J.B. Johnson, took her on a tour of the Minnesota State Capitol. Walking through the grand halls, Ethel found herself captivated by the building's sense of purpose. When she casually mentioned that she wouldn't mind working in such an environment, Mr. Johnson encouraged her to return to Duluth, reach out to her district representative, and apply for a position in the next legislative session.

Determined to act on his advice, Ethel went back to Duluth and took the Minnesota Civil Service exam. Her efforts paid off when, in January 1923, she became the first Black stenographer in the Minnesota State Legislature. It was a groundbreaking achievement, one that signified both personal success and broader progress for Black professionals.

Her role placed her in the heart of Minnesota's legislative process. Assigned to the Committees on Education, Banks and

Banking, and Apportionment, she observed firsthand the intricacies of policy making. The experience provided her with a deeper understanding of the institutional challenges Black Americans faced and expanded her network among those shaping laws.

Despite the prestige of her appointment, Ethel's presence in the legislature was met with curiosity and, at times, skepticism. Most of her colleagues were relatives of representatives, hired through nepotism, while she had earned her position through merit. This distinction set her apart. However, she refused to let doubt or discrimination deter her. At the close of the legislative session, her exceptional performance led to her retention as a court reporter for an investigation into the State Fish and Game Department.

The job was demanding. Her days were spent taking shorthand at hearings, and her evenings were devoted to transcribing notes. Fortunately, she had the unwavering support of Ida Mae Murphy, who ensured she ate properly and got adequate rest. The extra income enabled Ethel to start a bank account, offering her newfound financial independence. Yet, the relentless workload left her exhausted. The pressure of proving herself, of justifying the faith others had placed in her, was an ever-present burden.

Still, her experiences in the Minnesota Legislature laid the foundation for what would come next. Her work had opened doors, and those doors would soon lead her to an even broader stage.

Colored Girl Is Appointed Clerk In Legislature

Miss Ethel M. Ray of Duluth, daughter of Mr. and Mrs. W. H. Ray of Duluth, has been selected as one of the committee clerks in the legislature. Miss Ray is an efficient stenographer and typist, having served as stenographer two years during the settlement of the Moose Lake fire claims.

She was rated 100% for efficiency and courtesy upon inspection and has been assigned to three important committees. Several requests were made for her services. Miss Ray is an attractive young lady of very refined manners and a credit to her race.

The Minnesota Messenger, Minneapolis, MN, January 20, 1923

Ethel's bond with Mrs. Murphy was rooted in their shared triumphs over racial barriers. While Ethel opened doors for Black employment at the Minnesota State Capitol, Mrs. Murphy had become the first Black at a railway office in St. Paul. Their mutual experiences created a strong connection. Despite her success, Ethel sought new opportunities beyond Minnesota. Just a day after starting her job at the Minnesota Legislature on January 8, 1923, Ethel wrote to F.T. Lane, whom she had met during her 1919 trip with her father. Lane, then the Executive Secretary of the Community Service Urban

League in Kansas City, had ties to the YMCA in Chicago. Ethel's letter inquiring about job prospects in Kansas City reflected her ambition to advance her career and continue breaking barriers.

> 1854 Thomas Street,
> St. Paul, Minnesota,
> January 8th, 1923.
>
> Mr. F. T. Lane, Executive Secretary,
> Community Service Urban League,
> Kansas City, Missouri.
>
> Dear Mr. Lane:
>
> I have yours of recent date regarding a position in your office.
>
> I will be twenty-four years old next April. Have been working steady as stenographer for the past five years, and before that while in High School, did extra work after school and evenings. I worked under Col. H. V. Eva, Duluth, Minnesota, who was Chairman of the Minnesota Relief Commission, after the forest fires of 1918, and later for Charles F. Mahnke, Moose Lake, Minnesota. Did some extra work for R. D. Fox, Custom Officer, Post Office, Duluth.
>
> Under the Relief Commission, I came in contact with experienced social service workers from Chicago, New York and Boston. That was my introduction to "case work." I held interviews when not occupied otherwise—had charge of ordering office supplies part of the time during my work with the Commission also.
>
> Mr. Charles F. Mahnke had charge of the Relief work at Moose Lake, and my duties along that line were similar to what I did in Duluth. Mr. Mahnke was also Clerk of the School Board which necessitated the keeping of school records, issuing teachers' warrants, etc. He was Secretary-Treasurer of the Local Association of the Federal Farm Land Bank of St. Paul, which meant filing applications, drawing of legal papers, closing of loans, etc. When I first went to Moose Lake, Mr. Mahnke was owner and editor of the local newspaper which naturally gave me experience along that line. He specialized

A Seat at the Table: Ethel Ray Nance & the Harlem Renaissance

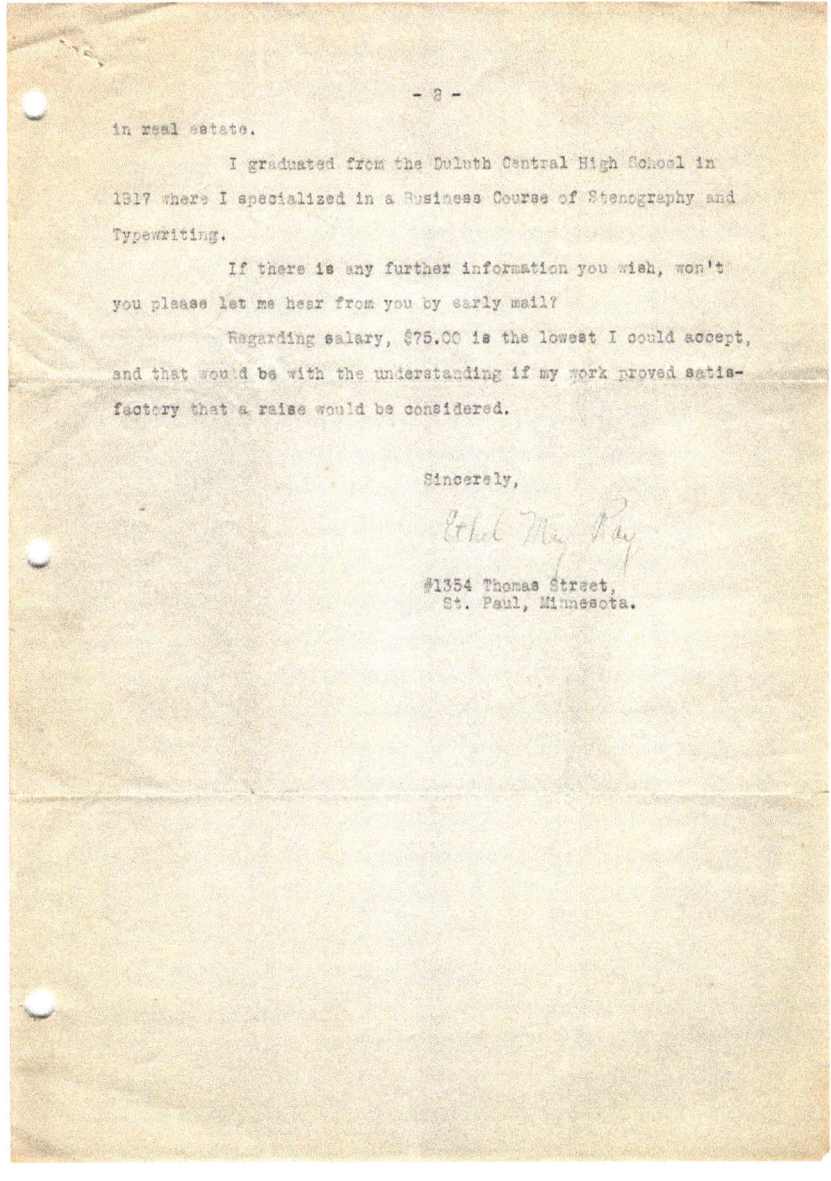

- 2 -

in real estate.

    I graduated from the Duluth Central High School in 1917 where I specialized in a Business Course of Stenography and Typewriting.

    If there is any further information you wish, won't you please let me hear from you by early mail?

    Regarding salary, $75.00 is the lowest I could accept, and that would be with the understanding if my work proved satisfactory that a raise would be considered.

                  Sincerely,

                    Ethel May Ray

                  #1354 Thomas Street,
                    St. Paul, Minnesota.

Ethel wrote to her parents on January 11, 1923, without mentioning her letter to F. T. seeking employment in Kansas City:

Thursday Morning, January 11th, 1923.

Dear Folks:

Well, this begins my Third Day in the Capitol, so I guess that's good news. Have been pretty tired in the evenings as yet, because we put in real days--lots of work and we keep at it steady, but I don't object to that. There are about ten of us--four or five are married, and the rest are along in years-- there is one probably about my age. One is a wife of a Representative, and so forth.

The head stenographer is daughter of the Speaker of the House, Miss Nolan(Now married and Mrs. BaDour). She is considerate to work under and works along herself. We each have a desk to ourself and take work from any of the Representatives. I have had some work from Mr. Lockhart. He told me yesterday I was already making my mark. Also said he wanted to know how I was getting along and if anything unpleasant came up, to let him know it and he would have me switched to a Committee. Had a chance of being placed on a Committee, but would rather stay here at least for a while because it gives you a chance to become acquainted with all kinds of bills, etc., so it would make it easier to change later. Not all of the "girls" take dictation.

A Seat at the Table: Ethel Ray Nance & the Harlem Renaissance

- 2 -

Everyone is tickled about my getting placed down here, and it's a puzzle as to just who is to be given the credit because everyone was working. Ribenack said I was slated for the Senate when Mr. Lockhart informed them I was already in the House. The salary is the same so I don't care-- $6.00 per day. Hours from 9 to 5 and an hour and a quarter for lunch. Go home for lunch so far as the street car fare is cheaper than to buy lunch, and I don't care about carrying lunch yet--may later.

A man spoke to me yesterday saying he heard Mr. Mahnke had several stenographers since I left. Upon inquiry found he was from Barnum. He is Assistant Sergant - at -Arms in the House.

Hoage and Mr. Smith and Mrs. Foster are now looking for something permanent after the Legislature is over. Am enclosing a Journal showing on the last page my appointment at the very top.

Feeling good now that most of the worry about getting placed is over.

Hope you are all well.

So long,

Ethel

F.T. Lane responded to Ethel's letter on February 7, 1923:

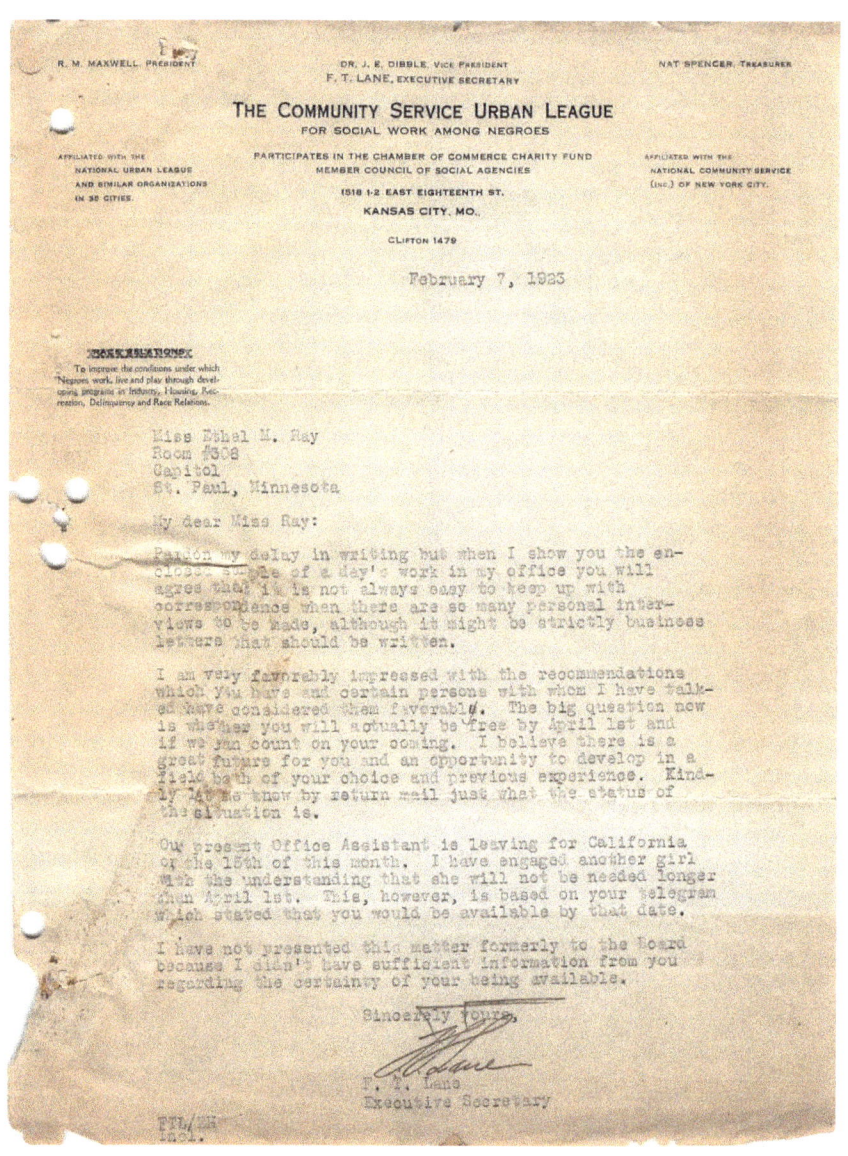

A Seat at the Table: Ethel Ray Nance & the Harlem Renaissance

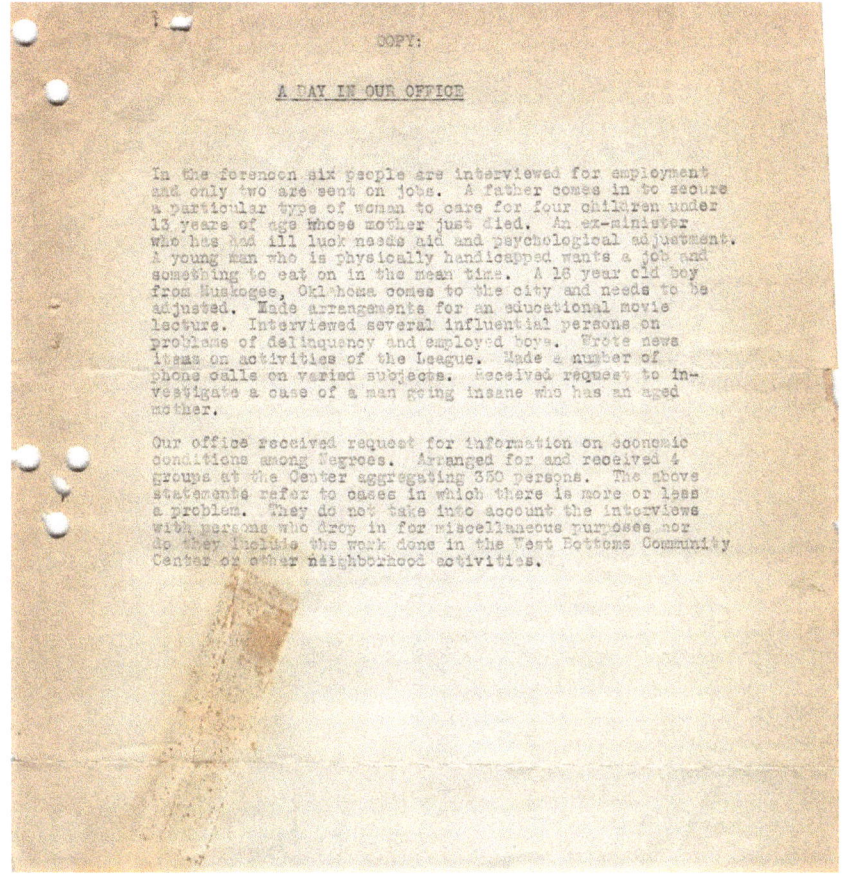

COPY:

A DAY IN OUR OFFICE

In the forenoon six people are interviewed for employment and only two are sent on jobs. A father comes in to secure a particular type of woman to care for four children under 13 years of age whose mother just died. An ex-minister who has had ill luck needs aid and psychological adjustment. A young man who is physically handicapped wants a job and something to eat on in the mean time. A 16 year old boy from Muskogee, Oklahoma comes to the city and needs to be adjusted. Made arrangements for an educational movie lecture. Interviewed several influential persons on problems of delinquency and employed boys. Wrote news items on activities of the League. Made a number of phone calls on varied subjects. Received request to investigate a case of a man going insane who has an aged mother.

Our office received request for information on economic conditions among Negroes. Arranged for and received 4 groups at the Center aggregating 350 persons. The above statements refer to cases in which there is more or less a problem. They do not take into account the interviews with persons who drop in for miscellaneous purposes nor do they include the work done in the West Bottoms Community Center or other neighborhood activities.

Chapter 6. When the World Came to Kansas City: The Birthplace of the Harlem Renaissance

Following her tenure in the Minnesota Legislature, a new opportunity emerged. In May 1923, Ethel accepted a position with the Community Service Urban League in Kansas City, Missouri, under the leadership of F.T. Lane. She was tasked with overseeing the employment department and community center, marking the beginning of her journey as a professional advocate for Black economic advancement.

Lane, who had known Ethel's father, recalled their time together in Chicago. He had witnessed William Henry Ray's stern but loving guidance and his determination to expose Ethel to history and intellectual growth. Now, Lane saw an opportunity to support Ethel's continued development, offering her a role in an organization dedicated to racial progress.

Kansas City provided an ideal environment for Ethel's ambitions. The city was a thriving hub of Black culture, intellectualism, and activism. However, discrimination remained a formidable barrier. As a young Black woman navigating new terrain, she faced obstacles that required both resilience and ingenuity. She quickly established a reputation for her precision and reliability as a stenographer, earning respect in spaces where Black women were often marginalized.

A Seat at the Table: Ethel Ray Nance & the Harlem Renaissance

Her work with the Urban League focused on employment advocacy, particularly for Black youth. In an era where job opportunities for young Black men were largely confined to positions at the YMCA or menial labor, Ethel developed programs that emphasized skills training and mentorship. Her initiatives not only empowered the youth but also challenged local businesses to reconsider their hiring practices. The praise she received from both Black and white leaders underscored her ability to bridge divides in the pursuit of social progress.

Kansas City also placed her at the center of significant national conversations. In October 1923, the Urban League held its annual meeting in the city. During the conference, Ethel met Eric Walrond, a prominent Afro-Caribbean writer and journalist deeply involved in the Harlem Renaissance. Their discussions left a lasting impression on her, foreshadowing her eventual connection to the movement.

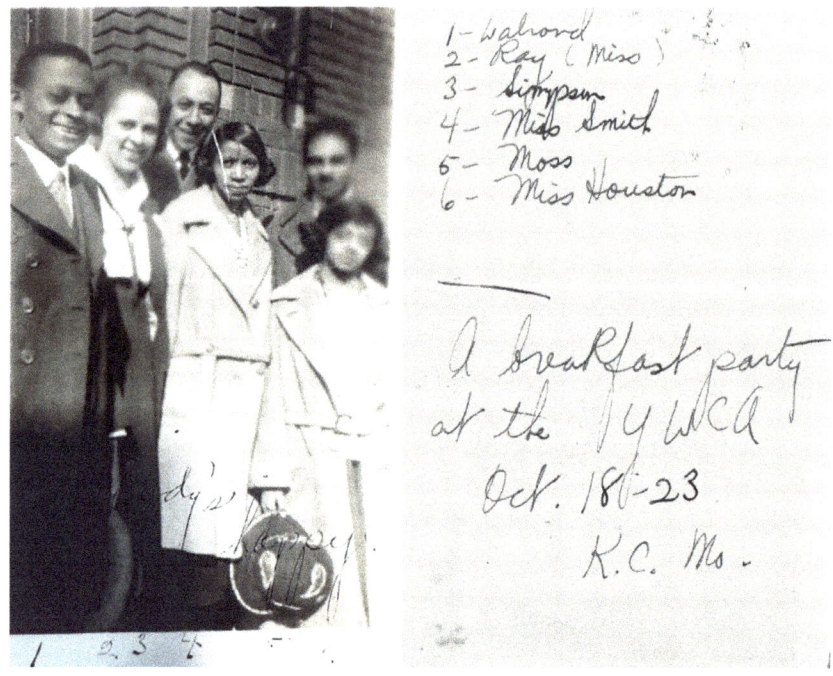

Words written on the photo: "Everybody's happy!" The bottom of the photo is numbered 1-6. Back of photo: "A breakfast party at the YWCA Oct. 18-23 K.C. Mo." Individuals: 1) Eric Waldron; 2) Ethel Ray Nance; 3) Simpson; 4) Miss Smith; 5) R. Maurice Moss; 6) Miss Houston.

A Seat at the Table: Ethel Ray Nance & the Harlem Renaissance

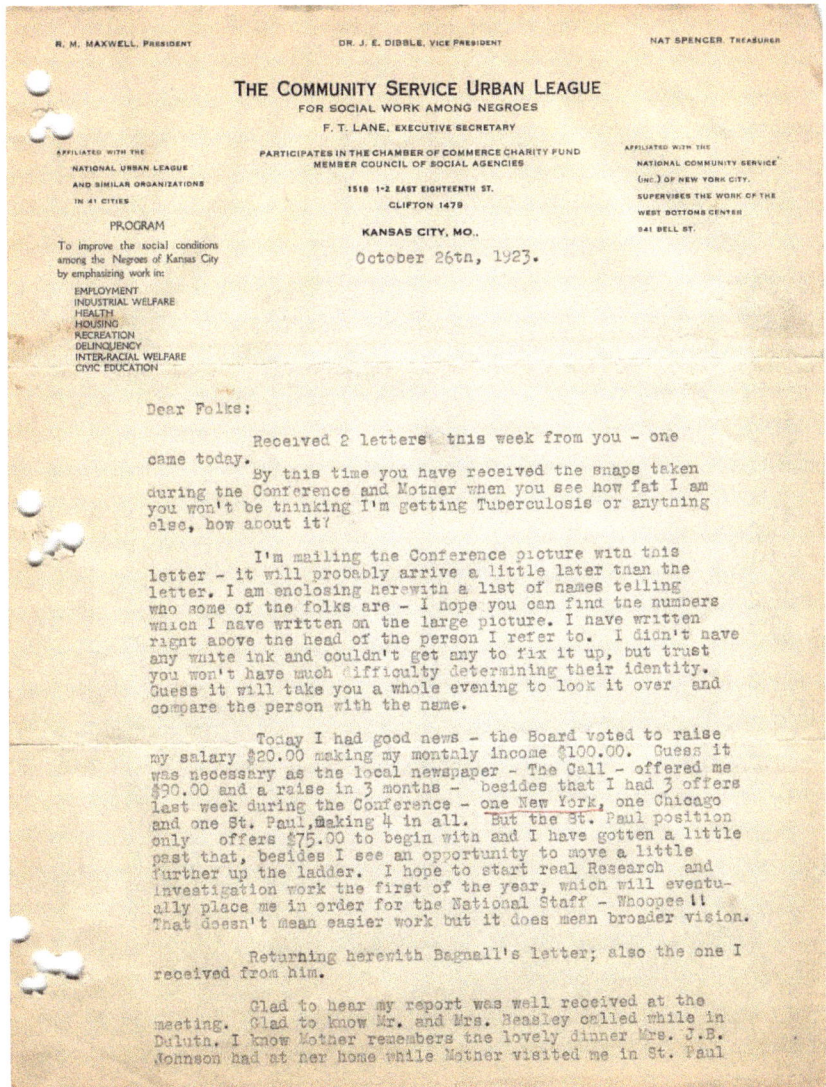

R. M. MAXWELL, PRESIDENT · DR. J. E. DIBBLE, VICE PRESIDENT · NAT SPENCER, TREASURER

THE COMMUNITY SERVICE URBAN LEAGUE
FOR SOCIAL WORK AMONG NEGROES
F. T. LANE, EXECUTIVE SECRETARY

AFFILIATED WITH THE
NATIONAL URBAN LEAGUE
AND SIMILAR ORGANIZATIONS
IN 41 CITIES

PARTICIPATES IN THE CHAMBER OF COMMERCE CHARITY FUND
MEMBER COUNCIL OF SOCIAL AGENCIES
1518 1-2 EAST EIGHTEENTH ST.
CLIFTON 1479

AFFILIATED WITH THE
NATIONAL COMMUNITY SERVICE
(INC.) OF NEW YORK CITY.
SUPERVISES THE WORK OF THE
WEST BOTTOMS CENTER
241 BELL ST.

PROGRAM
To improve the social conditions
among the Negroes of Kansas City
by emphasizing work in:
EMPLOYMENT
INDUSTRIAL WELFARE
HEALTH
HOUSING
RECREATION
DELINQUENCY
INTER-RACIAL WELFARE
CIVIC EDUCATION

KANSAS CITY, MO.,

October 26th, 1923.

Dear Folks:

Received 2 letters this week from you - one came today.

By this time you have received the snaps taken during the Conference and Mother when you see how fat I am you won't be thinking I'm getting Tuberculosis or anything else, how about it?

I'm mailing the Conference picture with this letter - it will probably arrive a little later than the letter. I am enclosing herewith a list of names telling who some of the folks are - I hope you can find the numbers which I have written on the large picture. I have written right above the head of the person I refer to. I didn't have any white ink and couldn't get any to fix it up, but trust you won't have much difficulty determining their identity. Guess it will take you a whole evening to look it over and compare the person with the name.

Today I had good news - the Board voted to raise my salary $20.00 making my monthly income $100.00. Guess it was necessary as the local newspaper - The Call - offered me $90.00 and a raise in 3 months - besides that I had 3 offers last week during the Conference - one New York, one Chicago and one St. Paul, making 4 in all. But the St. Paul position only offers $75.00 to begin with and I have gotten a little past that, besides I see an opportunity to move a little further up the ladder. I hope to start real Research and Investigation work the first of the year, which will eventually place me in order for the National Staff - Whoopee!! That doesn't mean easier work but it does mean broader vision.

Returning herewith Bagnall's letter; also the one I received from him.

Glad to hear my report was well received at the meeting. Glad to know Mr. and Mrs. Beasley called while in Duluth. I know Mother remembers the lovely dinner Mrs. J.B. Johnson had at her home while Mother visited me in St. Paul

- 2 -

Mrs. Beasley was over there too.

Glad Prof. William's recital was a success. I haven't Madaline's Burton's address - if you will get it for me I will drop her a line.

It was so funny during the Conference - both of you would have enjoyed it - Mr. S. S. Spaulding, the rich insurance man from Durham thought he remembered meeting me while in Durham when I mentioned the fact that I had visited there. I know very well I didn't meet him, but it seems his secretary is getting married and I guess he was looking out for another. Mr. Charles S. Johnson, Editor of Opportunity and Director of Research and Investigation of the National Urban League said to Lane: "All the people attending the Conference seem to be finding they need your Miss Ray on their particular staff." Ha, ha - it was so funny.

I have entered a Sociology class on Wednesday evenings which is under the supervision of Kansas University. Unlike the local schools, the class consists of both white and colored students, most of whom are teachers - so far out of 25 there are about 3 colored - Mr. E. J. Untnank is also taking the course. Hope to get a good deal out of it. It will help me in my work.

Mr. Attwell, Director of Community Service, who I mentioned had been here a couple of weeks ago, said anytime I thought it would be wise to talk "community work" there I should write him at Philadelphia. I wonder if a Community Service Urban League - like we have here - wouldn't be a good thing for Duluth. It is necessary for local people to write saying they are interested in such a thing. I believe you said your Charity Drive was over. It might be a good idea to get in touch with E. T. Attwell, 413 South Broad Street, Philadelphia. He will send you some literature and tell you how to proceed. The colored people will feel like giving more toward the Community Chest if they see where they are getting some direct benefit. Of course the one thing they are going to say is it will encourage segregation. That is an unfortunate truth perhaps, but those folks at Gary especially, should have some kind of Center. It is a question just where would be the best place for it. I would say have the headquarters out there because there the most of the people are located, then the secretary could work up our way also. We do a great deal of neighborhood work here going into various neighborhoods surroundingx around the city. You might say to Attwell that I suggested that you write him. Of course he will want a Community Service Organization altogether, and the Urban League folks will want an Urban League altogether, but I believe the field is best suited to the combined—that will give you the employment work; will give the secretary a chance to form clubs, etc. among the steel plant men, and act as a medium between them and the employers. We had two or three white steel farxx men from Pittsburgh here for the Conference

(Missing page 3)

A Seat at the Table: Ethel Ray Nance & the Harlem Renaissance

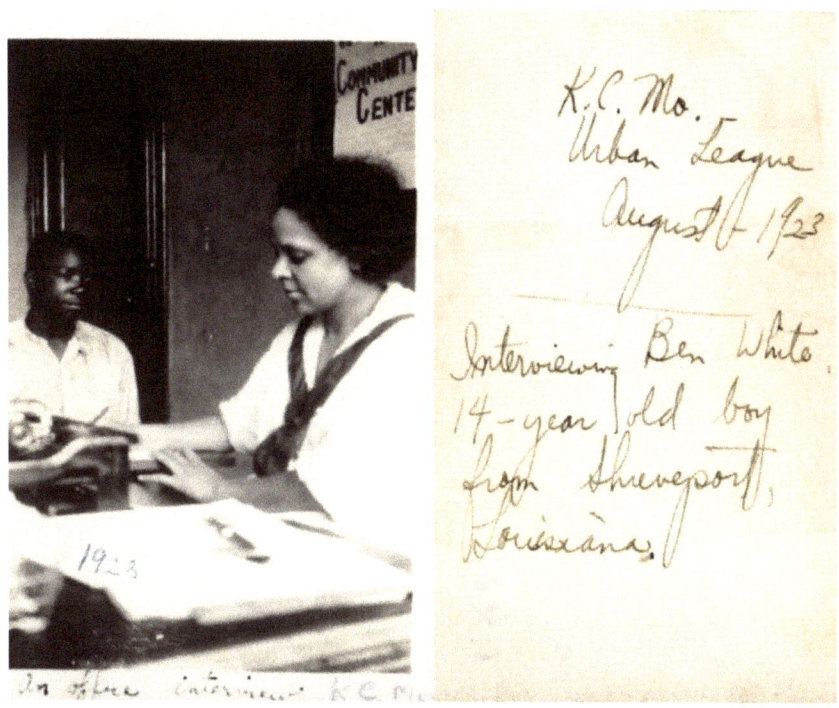

1923: An office interview. K.C.,Mo. Back of photo: K.C., Mo. Urban League August 1923-Interviewing Ben White, 14-year-old boy From Shreveport, Louisiana

"And Along Came Ben"
By ETHEL MAY RAY

HE made a pathetic picture when he shambled into our office one morning, not overly clean, dressed in a nondescript cap, shirt and pair of trousers, with another old cap pushed half way down into a back pocket. His lip was badly swollen and the right eye nearly closed.

During the interview he fingered the cap which he had been wearing. In his slow manner of speech we learned he had "beaten" his way from a small town in Louisiana where he had been living with his mother's parents; that he could neither read nor write; that he believed himself 18 years old—in reality he is about 15. He was looking for work—"I can do mos' anything."

Upon inquiry as to the cause of the injured eye and lip, it came out that there had been a fight with some boys about a cap he had found—he pointed to the cap in his back pocket. After treating the injuries and feeding him, odd jobs about the Center were done in return.

He proved very willing, apt, truthful, and unusually fond of headgear. Every few days another cap or hat would appear that he had found, picked up or bought from a man for "two-bits." Extreme care was taken of these new possessions—they were brushed and dusted carefully in spare moments. He was given some old clothing which he took fairly good care of—and he talked of the time when he would get a whole suit of clothing—a coat too. He had been to school a few days, it seems, but had forgotten how to write his name. One day, after setting a copy before him to practice on, he brought in a slip of paper with the word "FOX" printed and said: "That's what my grandpa calls my uncle." He had remembered this word and knew what it meant. He was willing to learn to write and kept at it quite steadily, only falling asleep once while so occupied. He was familiar with money and seemed to have no difficulty in counting change.

After he had been with us about a week, one day without any warning he "burst forth" into song—one of those plaintive croons or blues of southern plantations—we decided it was from sheer happiness, however, and not loneliness—he never appeared sad and said he didn't want to return home.

He had a peculiar way of moving quickly now and then. I can't understand yet whether it was his first experience on the second floor of a building or what made him do this particular thing—nevertheless, often he would come into a room, cross quickly to a window, push it up as far as it would go, and lean way out—so far out that only half of his body remained in the room. The first time he did this, the incident was breath-taking—I expected to see the rest of him disappear also. Perhaps it was the novelty of looking down on the busy street of passing people, racing automobiles and noisy, clanging street cars.

After a month's stay with us, we found a home with a couple who had no children and who wished to give him a home, clothing and an opportunity for school in exchange for assistance with the man's janitor work in an apartment. They got in touch with us through a notice in the local paper that a "Big Brother" was needed.

He drops in to see us frequently and is happy. He is always dressed very, very neatly—has two or three suits now—wears a collar and tie all of the time—keeps his shoes shined nicely, and along with the outward transformation it seems he has lost most of his original shamble. I mustn't omit the fact that the once kinky hair is now straight, glossy and slick. He is enthusiastic about night school and informs us that he is "learning nearly everything."

In the meantime we notified his relatives of his whereabouts and his grandfather requested his return, but it didn't seem quite fair to send him back to a life of darkness just when he had the door of opportunity opened to him, and when he is eagerly making the most of his chance to learn.

During the Christmas season, the time of year when all wanderers wish for home and relatives—he went to Louisiana, but not to stay.

Ben is only one of the many young fellows whom the Community Service Urban League of Kansas City, Missouri, has helped during the year.

The following year, Kansas City became an unexpected hub of intellectual and cultural exchange, hosting both the National Urban League and the National Conference of Social Workers' annual meetings. These gatherings attracted prominent figures from across the country, fostering collaboration and innovation in fields of social work and Black community advancement. Leaders from major cities like New York, Chicago, and Philadelphia convened to exchange strategies and build national networks aimed at advancing racial and economic progress.

Stationed at the reception desk, Ethel became the face of the Kansas City Urban League, greeting and assisting hundreds of attendees. Her professionalism, efficiency, and charismatic presence left a lasting impression on the nation's leading educators, civil servants, and publishers. As a result, she received multiple job offers, further solidifying her reputation as a rising force in the movement for racial and social justice.

The significance of Kansas City as the birthplace of the Renaissance lies in the serendipitous convergence of these figures and the intellectual energy generated during the Urban League and National Conference of Social Workers meetings. As Ethel later reflected, "The world came to Kansas City," and with it came the seeds of a movement that would forever change American culture.

Kansas City, Mo.-Urban League, 1924: Ethel is seated in the middle of the front row.

It was also in Kansas City that Ethel formed a pivotal connection with Aaron Douglas, a young art teacher at Lincoln High School, and William L. Dawson, a talented musician. She frequently dined at the same small restaurant where they would gather, deep in conversation over books and artistic aspirations. Ethel often encouraged Douglas and Dawson to explore opportunities beyond Kansas City. Douglas expressed his ambition to study art in Paris, while Ethel countered with the advantages of New York's burgeoning Black arts scene. Johnson soon tasked her with convincing Douglas to move to Harlem, where his work could flourish. Ethel's instincts proved correct—Douglas eventually relocated to New York and became one of the most celebrated visual artists of the Harlem Renaissance.

However, New York beckoned.

A letter from Charles S. Johnson outlined an opportunity too significant to ignore. He described a position at *Opportunity* requiring someone with a sharp mind for research, an eye for storytelling, and the ability to shape narratives that would drive the national conversation on Black identity and progress. The job would grant her access to an invaluable archive of materials on Black migration and social change—resources that could form the foundation of a book.

"Everything centers in New York," Johnson wrote.

For Ethel, navigating this tension was both a professional challenge and a personal revelation. She admired Du Bois for his intellectual brilliance and commitment to justice, yet she was drawn to Johnson's belief in cultural expression as a form of activism.

Charles S. Johnson, the editor of *Opportunity: Journal of Negro Life*, was a rising star within the National Urban League and a visionary who believed in the transformative power of Black art and literature. Johnson saw *Opportunity* as more than a magazine; he saw it as the intellectual engine of a cultural movement. Impressed by Ethel's organizational acumen and commitment to justice, he extended her a personal invitation to join his team in New York as a researcher.

The rivalry between *The Crisis*, edited by W.E.B. Du Bois, and *Opportunity* was about more than being published; it was about two different visions for advancing the Black community.

The Crisis, founded in 1910 as the NAACP's official magazine, was a powerhouse of political thought, addressing civil rights, racial violence, and inequality head-on. Under Du Bois's leadership, the magazine became the definitive voice for activism, publishing essays, reports on lynchings, and literary works that reinforced the urgent need for systemic change. Du Bois's editorials carried his unmistakable voice, forceful, brilliant, and often uncompromising. He saw Black excellence as a means to prove racial equality, but he believed that this excellence had to be tethered to direct political confrontation.

In contrast, *Opportunity* was a celebration of Black cultural identity through art and literature. Founded in 1923 by the National Urban League, it quickly gained traction for its annual literary contests and cultural focus. Johnson believed that beauty and storytelling could combat prejudice in ways that policy alone could not. While *The Crisis* showcased literary works within a larger framework of political discourse, *Opportunity* made Black art and literature its primary focus, elevating stories, poetry, and visual art as vehicles of empowerment. Johnson's aim was to position Black artists as intellectual leaders worthy of patronage and national recognition. This philosophical divide created a friendly but palpable rivalry between the two publications.

Du Bois respected Johnson's literary achievements but was wary of his collaborations with white benefactors and his focus on art over activism. Du Bois feared that emphasizing culture alone could overshadow the need for direct action against systemic racism. To Johnson, however, the arts were not a distraction but a vital strategy for reimagining Black identity.

For Ethel, navigating this tension was both a professional challenge and a personal revelation. She admired Du Bois for his intellectual brilliance and commitment to justice, yet she was drawn to Johnson's belief in cultural expression as a form of activism. When Johnson invited her to work for *Opportunity*, Ethel sought guidance from F.T. Lane. Lane, ever humorous, responded, "I don't want your father hunting me down if he doesn't approve."

Ethel wrote in her diary: "I felt I was just getting accustomed to Kansas City and its large Black population, and the little gal from the country was a bit slow at attacking a larger city right away. I knew my parents would veto such a decision. I kept quite close touch with home, my father encouraging me to write home about my experiences. I am duly thankful to him for his foresight in this since my letters to him, together with bits of my diary, help make more vivid some of my experiences in Harlem later on."

Part III: A Journey to Harlem

Chapter 7. Harlem Bound: Arriving in the Heart of a Movement

In May 1924, at the age of 25, Ethel Ray Nance boarded a train from Kansas City to Harlem, New York. The Harlem she arrived in was alive with cultural vibrancy and intellectual energy, a stark contrast to the quiet streets of Duluth and the segregated neighborhoods of Kansas City. Harlem had become the epicenter of a burgeoning movement—what would later be called the Harlem Renaissance—where Black artists, writers, and activists were reshaping cultural and social norms.

The conferences in Kansas City reinforced Ethel's belief in the power of cultural and intellectual exchange, and Charles S. Johnson's offer to work at Opportunity magazine presented an opportunity she could not ignore. With the support of the Urban League and the encouragement of figures like Johnson and Eric Walrond, she knew that New York was where she needed to be. Ultimately, Ethel chose to follow her ambition and accepted Johnson's offer. To avoid potential conflicts, she made the decision to move without first informing her parents or Dr. W.E.B. Du Bois. When she did, she framed the transition as a promotion, emphasizing that she was being transferred to the National Urban League office in New York. Her father, William Henry Ray, remained apprehensive but took comfort in knowing that influential figures like Du Bois and A. Philip Randolph were in the city. With Du Bois frequently traveling, Randolph assumed an informal role as her guardian.

Despite her efforts, Ethel's decision caught Du Bois by surprise. Upon hearing of her move, he wrote to her father, asking, "Why wasn't I told?" William Henry Ray, equally surprised, replied, "I didn't know either." The exchange underscored Ethel's independent spirit; she was carving her own path on her own terms.

On May 14, 1924, Ethel arrived in New York City, where she was greeted at Grand Central Station by Madeline Allison, Charles S. Johnson, and Eric Walrond. Allison, a writer and editor for The Crisis from 1911 to 1922, was working as a writer for *Opportunity* in 1924. Walrond, a published novelist and business manager for *Opportunity*, had maintained a friendship with Ethel since their time in Kansas City. The trio welcomed Ethel into Harlem's transformative cultural milieu.

Harlem's bustling streets, crowded tenements, and vibrant energy overwhelmed yet invigorated Ethel. Finding housing proved challenging due to racial and gender discrimination, but she eventually secured a room with Regina Anderson (later Regina Andrews), a librarian and cultural luminary. Regina's apartment at 580 St. Nicholas Avenue became Ethel's sanctuary and the starting point of her journey into Harlem's intellectual and artistic community.

Ethel's letters to her family conveyed her awe at the city's electric atmosphere. The 135th Street Library became her gateway to Harlem's intellectual debates on race, art, and politics. She was no longer merely an observer of history; she was now shaping it, standing at the center of a movement that would redefine the cultural landscape of Black America.

A Seat at the Table: Ethel Ray Nance & the Harlem Renaissance

L. HOLLINGSWORTH WOOD, Chairman
EUGENE KINCKLE JONES, Executive Secretary
CHARLES S. JOHNSON, Editor

OPPORTUNITY

PUBLISHED BY
The Department of Research and Investigations
NATIONAL URBAN LEAGUE
127 EAST 23rd STREET, NEW YORK CITY
Telephone Gramercy : 3978

WILLIAM H. BALDWIN, Secretary
A. S. FRISSELL, Treasurer

PAUL G. PRAYER, Business Manager

May 30th, 1924.

Dear Folks:

    Well, I'm able by this time to go and come to work without getting lost - however, I've never been lost because of the kindness of Miss Allison who lives right across the street from me, and the first few mornings she picked me up at the Y.W.C.A. on 137th Street where I eat breakfast. Now I come and go alone, and like the "being alone." I enjoy that most of all so far here - the feeling that it isn't necessary to be dependent on anyone. My work is more than interesting and don't have many interruptions - such a contrast from Moose Lake and Kansas City - there is a great deal to be done and I actually couldn't realize the immensity of this job - it's a position but it's a big job too. We, as the Research Department, must be the food for the magazine and be the source of any information/for any of the 37 to 40 branches of the Urban League over the country, but Mr. Johnson is an excellent character, and seems to feel I will fit the job. In fact the way he outlined his plans to me a few days ago, it nearly scared me because it seems they are making a position that will make it impossible for me to ever get away - ha ha - but time enough to worry about that at a later date, now my work's the thing.

A JOURNAL OF NEGRO LIFE

OPPORTUNITY

PUBLISHED BY
The Department of Research and Investigations
NATIONAL URBAN LEAGUE
127 EAST 23rd STREET, NEW YORK CITY
Telephone Gramercy : 3978

L. HOLLINGSWORTH WOOD, Chairman
EUGENE KINCKLE JONES, Executive Secretary
CHARLES S. JOHNSON, Editor
WILLIAM H. BALDWIN, Secretary
A. S. FRISSELL, Treasurer
PAUL G. PRAYER, Business Manager

- 2 -

Yesterday, monday, was my first day to receive mail so it made me feel that I was still in this world and hadn't shipped off anywhere to a desert island - rather a comfortable feeling. Today I find 2 more letters that you forwarded from home. By the way I got 8 letters yesterday.

The weather here is more like Duluth - cool yet pleasant, and the nights have been splendid.

Our department is on the 5th floor - the National secretary is on the 3rd floor - I'm glad we are off by ourselves. We have a force of 6 - Mr. Taylor, Business Manager, his secretary Miss Bowser; then there's Miss Allison who works on the magazine collecting news, and sees to having the information put in the magazine; then Miss Earl a stenographer, and your honorable daughter and Mr. Johnson. I' haven't learned my title yet, but it's a new position seemingly they are creating - my desk is due to arrive today.

I've heard that the Defender ran my picture last week - will see a copy today. Lord, if I had realized the bigness of this position I might have not been so ready to allow all the publicity in the Western papers. But it's pleasant to come into a new community and

A JOURNAL OF NEGRO LIFE

A Seat at the Table: Ethel Ray Nance & the Harlem Renaissance

Miss Ethel May Ray, Chicago Defender, May 17, 1924

sort of "start over." I am staying by myself and
Thomas's I find, do not bother me. I go home and
can shut myself in. My room is large and comfortable
and clean. And being the only roomer makes a difference - I have little privileges like pressing, washing
out a few things, etc. Mrs. Thomas is very motherly
but so far hasn't been bothersome at all.

It is pleasant to feel alone as I said before.
I go along 7th Avenue and Lenox Avenues and can feel
that I owe nothing particularly and I rather enjoy
not feeling I must look for someone I know for fear
I may pass them by without speaking. My work absorbs
every bit of me just now. Our hours are from 9 to 5
but I don't work by a clock exactly - it makes one
hurry too much. I finish up what I think should be
done, and then go home - because my predominant desire
here is the work. Social life can come later - and I'm
not strong on that anyhow. I have had invitations to
dances and parties already but have turned them down
saying I'm not accepting invitations yet due to my
work, etc. These have been nice affairs - invited
through the workers at the Y.W.C.A., etc. but I don't
want to get under obligations so early, because they
certainly feel that you are - I know that, so am
paying my way and travelling slowly.

Saturday afternoon, we have off - I staid

- 4 -

to do a little work and Walrond, the novelist and magazine writer, came by the office and we walked part way home. Walked from 23rd Street along 5th Avenue to 72nd Street. Passed the Wahdorf-Astoria, etc. etc. I walk past Madison Square and the Metropolitan Life Building every day as I come to work on the Elevated and that is about 4 blocks away. Saturday we stopped in Central Park to rest-and fed peanuts to the pigeons, squirrels and sparrows that very quickly found what we were eating and came close to our bench. Saturday was a lovely day and the Park was rather restful.

I'm glad our office is down town - I shouldn't like to work in Harlem - if one lived and worked both in Harlem it would make your life too narrow.

Well, I've tried to mention my ideas on New York so far - one can't help but feel that here is everything in life one could possibly be looking for - that it is here and you must only look for it, and when you find it you may acquire it by paying the price.

I feel fine and feel settled - it does not seem possible I am very far away from Duluth, although I seem an awful distance from Kansas City - isn't that funny?

Love to all - am sending a few cards to let my friends in the West know I've arrived at "the end of the earth."

So long,

Ethel

Room 50-51
127 E. 23rd St.

New York in 1924 pulsed with creative energy, a cultural awakening that positioned Harlem as the epicenter of Black artistry, literature, and intellectual thought. Ethel stepped into this world through the doors of Opportunity magazine, where her first task was to assist in processing the flood of manuscripts from aspiring writers eager to contribute to the growing movement. Johnson had built *Opportunity* into more than a publication—it was a platform for rising Black talent, an engine propelling the Harlem Renaissance forward.

As Ethel settled into her role, she found herself immersed in conversations about race, identity, and progress—conversations that had the power to shape a new cultural narrative. Harlem, with its vibrant streets, jazz-filled nightclubs, and literary salons, became both her workplace and her home.

What had begun as a career move now felt like destiny. Ethel Ray Nance was not just witnessing the Harlem Renaissance—she was becoming a part of it. From the segregated streets of Duluth to the legislative halls of Minnesota, from the bustling activism of Kansas City to the heart of Harlem, Ethel had followed her calling. Now, she was poised to leave her mark—not just on the movement but on the very fabric of American history.

A Seat at the Table: Ethel Ray Nance & the Harlem Renaissance

Chapter 8. The Diabolical Ray: Ethel's Ties to Harlem's Luminaries

Photo of Ethel May Ray (Nance) Abt 1925

When Ethel Ray Nance arrived in New York City at the behest

of Charles S. Johnson, she stepped into the heart of a burgeoning cultural revolution. Harlem in the 1920s was alive with possibility. Writers, artists, musicians, and activists converged to create a vibrant community synonymous with creativity and resilience. Among them was Ethel, affectionately dubbed "The Diabolical Ray" by journalist L.H. Wood, managing editor of *The New York*

Amsterdam News. He was captivated by Ethel's fiery spirit and quick wit. The nickname, "The Diabolical Ray," highlighted her magnetic personality. Their relationship, marked by intellectual exchanges and playful banter, epitomized how Ethel's presence left a lasting impression on Harlem's cultural elite.

Ethel's arrival in Harlem was far from quiet. As one of the first Black stenographers at the National Urban League, she quickly became integral to the organization's operations. Her role placed her alongside influential figures like W.E.B. Du Bois, James Weldon Johnson, and Fauset Redmon Fauset. Beyond her professional contributions, Ethel's ability to forge deep, personal connections elevated her influence within Harlem's intellectual and cultural circles.

Her connection with Charles S. Johnson was particularly significant. Johnson, a strategic thinker, recognized Ethel's talents as a confidante and colleague. Together, they worked on initiatives that advanced Black art and literature while advocating for social justice. Ethel's understanding of the interconnectedness of culture and activism deepened through her work with Johnson.

Ethel's influence extended beyond her professional responsibilities. She became a fixture at Harlem's gatherings and salons, where luminaries like Langston Hughes, Zora Neale Hurston, and Countee Cullen debated the role of art in addressing racial injustice and fostering pride in Black identity. Ethel's Midwestern upbringing and experiences in Kansas City gave her a unique perspective that enriched these discussions.

A Seat at the Table: Ethel Ray Nance & the Harlem Renaissance

One of Ethel's most notable contributions was her mentorship of Aaron Douglas. True to her word, she encouraged Douglas to leave his teaching position in Kansas City and immerse himself in Harlem's creative scene. Ethel's persistent support and connections helped Douglas gain opportunities to showcase his art, culminating in his rise as a defining artist of the Harlem Renaissance. His Afrocentric modernist style became an iconic visual hallmark of the movement, and Ethel's role in his journey underscored her knack for nurturing talent.

Ethel's ability to foster connections and build community was evident in her relationship with Aaron Douglas. She worked tirelessly to secure him opportunities, even enlisting W.E.B. Du Bois' help to find Douglas a job at *The Crisis* Shipping department. Ethel's determination paid off when Douglas' art began to appear in prominent publications, launching his career.

L.H. Wood's playful moniker for Ethel reflected the respect and admiration she garnered in Harlem. Known for her strong opinions and ability to hold her own in intellectual debates, Ethel's dynamic personality resonated with those who knew her. Dr. L.M. Collins of Fisk University described her as a socialite of the Harlem Renaissance, a title Ethel modestly refuted. She described her community as one bound by shared success and mutual celebration rather than competition.

Interview of Ethel Ray Nance by Ann Allen Shockley: November 18 & December 23, 1970; pages 45-46:

Shockley: *One of our faculty, here at Fisk University, Dr. L. M. Collins, describes you to me as a socialite of the Harlem*

Renaissance Period, why do you think that he would give you this title?

Nance: *I can't imagine why the term socialite. We never regarded ourselves…in that light. We were all struggling, three of us girls had an apartment and…our salaries were not very high, but the rent was high. We couldn't do any lavish entertaining, but I think it was that with the younger people who were starting to write and draw, it was a place where they could drop in and they could meet others and it was a place where whenever anyone had a little success, any kind of success, or they were published or they'd had an interview…we'd get together and everybody would rejoice. I don't recall, there being…any instances of jealousy because one person was successful in getting in print and someone else had not been accepted. I think that was the thing that held us together, it was sort of…a little family, and if one had some success it seemed to…to be shared…with all of us. But, socialite, I don't…don't know…just who Dr. Collins might have talked to…to have gotten that impression because…I used to stay away from…social events as much as I possibly could, they were boring to me.*

Ethel's legacy is intertwined with the achievements of the Harlem Renaissance. Her relationships with luminaries like Langston Hughes, Zora Neale Hurston, and Aaron Douglas highlighted her role as a connector and advocate. As Harlem's cultural movement flourished, Ethel stood at its heart, her indomitable spirit and vision illuminating the path forward for generations to come.

Chapter 9: Dream Haven: A Cultural Oasis in Harlem

Ethel Ray Nance's apartment, shared with Regina Andrews and Luella Tucker, became a vibrant hub of creativity and camaraderie during the Harlem Renaissance. Nicknamed "Dream Haven," the space at 580 St. Nicholas Avenue served as a sanctuary where artists, writers, and intellectuals gathered to collaborate, celebrate successes, and exchange ideas. As David Levering Lewis aptly described:

"It served as a sort of Renaissance USO, offering a couch, a meal, sympathy, and a proper introduction to wicked Harlem for newcomers on the Urban League's approved list." Lewis, David Levering. When Harlem Was in Vogue. Alfred A. Knopf, 1981 (Lewis 127)

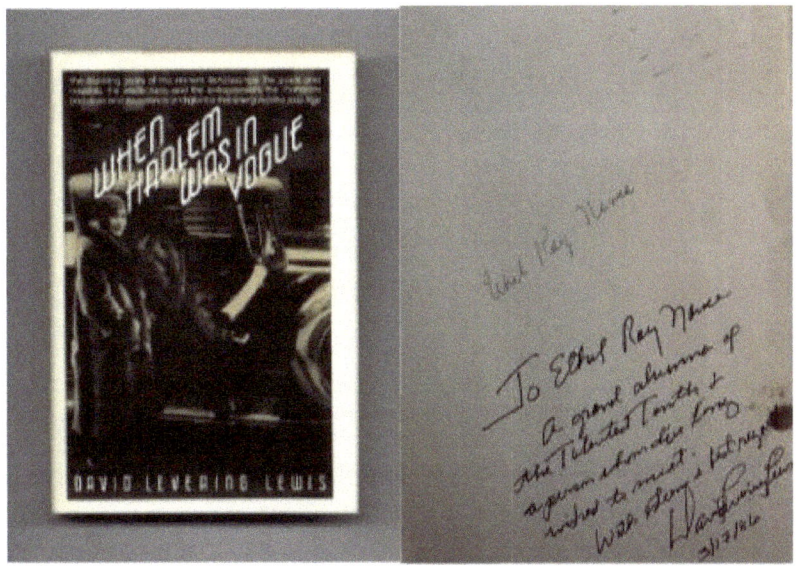

David Levering Lewis autographed Ethel's copy of his book, *"When Harlem Was in Vogue."* The inscription reads: "To Ethel Ray Nance, A grand alumna of the Talented Tenth & a person whom I've long wished to meet. With esteem & best regards, David Levering Lewis 3/17/86."

Together with their third roommate, Luella Tucker, the trio transformed their apartment into what became known as "Dream Haven." It was more than a residence; it was a sanctuary where ideas flourished, dreams took shape, and friendships forged new paths for cultural progress.

The atmosphere of Dream Haven was dynamic and inclusive. Regina Andrews, a librarian at the 135th Street Library, introduced Ethel to Harlem's most influential personalities, while Luella Tucker's warmth and organizational skills added structure to the household. Together, the trio hosted gatherings that were both planned and impromptu, creating a space where creative energy thrived. Frequent visitors included Langston Hughes, Countee Cullen, and Jean Toomer. Ethel fondly recalled in her diary how Cullen was going to the university in New York, preparing to graduate, and they saw him often.

"He was a very likeable person, very gentle, and frequently stopped by to share his latest poetry, saying, 'would you like to hear what I've written'" There was never a show of being egotistic or grandstanding, it was just, I think that he appreciated our friendship. He was always so unassuming and charming, a fine young man, and we were only too happy to have him come, whatever we were doing, we would stop and listen. "

Ethel and her roommates took Cullen to his first nightclub after he graduated from college, introducing him to Harlem's vibrant nightlife. Ethel admired Cullen's gentle and kind demeanor, noting that he never sought to overshadow others.

Langston Hughes was another regular guest, sometimes giving readings of his poetry.

Even W.E.B. Du Bois, despite his hectic schedule, made time to attend Dream Haven gatherings. Ethel recounted how his presence elevated the events: "I remember he was there when Langston Hughes returned from his long boat trip." Occasionally, Du Bois treated Ethel and her roommates to simple meals in Greenwich Village, enjoying hot dogs and allowing them a glass of beer.

The gatherings at Dream Haven were not limited to literary discussions. Notable figures such as Paul Robeson and Walter White frequently visited, adding their voices to the dynamic exchanges. Taxi drivers referred to the apartment as "the 580," a testament to its reputation as a cultural hotspot. Gloria T. Hull characterized the apartment as a "forum for meetings, people, and ideas," reflecting its significance as a creative and intellectual incubator.

Ethel's connection to the Urban League played a significant role in shaping the Renaissance. Through her work, she advocated for social and economic justice, empowering Black individuals and families. Her efforts to organize educational and recreational programs for Black youth nurtured a new generation of artists and thinkers. Additionally, her position in the Department of Research allowed her to analyze and document the Black experience, contributing valuable insights that informed the movement's cultural landscape.

Dream Haven's influence extended beyond its walls. The apartment became a microcosm of the Harlem Renaissance, where art, activism, and intellectual exploration converged. Luminaries like Zora Neale Hurston, Aaron Douglas, and Eric Walrond found inspiration within its walls. Ethel's mentorship of Aaron Douglas was particularly impactful; she encouraged him to leave Kansas City and join Harlem's artistic community, ultimately helping him secure opportunities that launched his career as a defining artist of the era.

Ethel's recollections of Dream Haven reveal its importance not only as a residence but as a cultural institution. "It was more than a home; it was a haven for intellectuals, artists, and writers who were shaping the future of Black culture in America," she said. The apartment's gatherings were marked by a spirit of mutual support and shared success. Ethel noted, "We never asked much of these young writers, and maybe that was one reason they liked being around us. We never placed them on exhibit; we just celebrated their successes together."

Dream Haven symbolized the transformative power of community during the Harlem Renaissance. It was within these walls that friendships flourished, movements were ignited, and the cultural narrative of the 20th century began to take shape. Ethel Ray Nance's role in creating and sustaining this space underscores her legacy as a connector, advocate, and visionary.

Ethel's connection to the Urban League played a significant role in shaping the Renaissance. Through her work, she advocated for social and economic justice, empowering Black individuals and families. Her efforts to organize educational and recreational programs for Black youth nurtured a new generation of artists and thinkers. Additionally, her position in the Department of Research allowed her to analyze and document the Black experience, contributing valuable insights that informed the movement's cultural landscape.

The trio's apartment also became a bridge between diverse communities. Carl Van Vechten, a white patron of the arts, was a regular visitor. While his intentions were sometimes questioned, Ethel and Regina strategically engaged with him to secure opportunities for Black artists while retaining control over their narrative. Their ability to balance collaboration with self-determination was emblematic of Dream Haven's ethos.

Dream Haven's influence extended beyond its walls. The apartment became a microcosm of the Harlem Renaissance, where art, activism, and intellectual exploration converged. Luminaries like Zora Neale Hurston, Aaron Douglas, and Eric Walrond found inspiration within its walls. Ethel's mentorship of Aaron Douglas was particularly impactful; she encouraged him to leave Kansas City and join Harlem's artistic community, ultimately helping him secure opportunities that launched his career as a defining artist of the era.

Ethel's recollections of Dream Haven reveal its importance not only as a residence but as a cultural institution. "It was more than a home; it was a haven for intellectuals, artists, and writers who were shaping the future of Black culture in America," she said. The apartment's gatherings were marked by a spirit of mutual support and shared success. Ethel noted, "We never asked much of these young writers, and maybe that was one reason they liked being around us. We never placed them on exhibit; we just celebrated their successes together."

Dream Haven symbolized the transformative power of community during the Harlem Renaissance. It was within these walls that friendships flourished, movements were ignited, and the cultural narrative of the 20th century began to take shape. Ethel Ray Nance's role in creating and sustaining this space underscores her legacy as a connector, advocate, and visionary.

In summary, Opportunity's events played a crucial role in shaping the Harlem Renaissance by fostering artistic collaboration, building community, elevating visibility, and engaging with important social issues, thereby contributing to the movement's lasting legacy.

Part IV: The Renaissance Unfolds

Chapter 10: The Opportunity Dinner

The Civic Club: March 21, 1925

On March 21, 1925, a momentous event took place in New York City that would leave an indelible mark on the literary and cultural landscape of America. The New York Writers Guild Dinner, hosted at the Civic Club and orchestrated by Charles S. Johnson, editor of *Opportunity: A Journal of Negro Life*, became a seminal moment in the Harlem Renaissance. This gathering of intellectuals, writers, and patrons celebrated the burgeoning literary talent within the African American community and symbolized the collective power of Black artistry in redefining cultural narratives.

Charles S. Johnson, a visionary leader and advocate for racial uplift, used his platform at *Opportunity* to spotlight African American achievements and confront systemic racism. By 1925, Harlem had already established itself as the epicenter of a cultural renaissance, attracting writers, musicians, and artists who sought to challenge societal limitations and express the complexities of Black life. The dinner was conceived as an opportunity to bring together established figures in the literary world and emerging Black writers. Johnson's aim was twofold: to provide a platform for African American talent to gain recognition in a predominantly white publishing industry and to foster connections that could lead to tangible support for their work. In this sense, the Civic Club dinner was not merely a social gathering but a deliberate act of cultural advocacy and strategic networking.

A Seat at the Table: Ethel Ray Nance & the Harlem Renaissance

The dinner's success was deeply influenced by a collaboration of key individuals who helped set the foundation for the Harlem Renaissance. Ethel Ray Nance, Charles S. Johnson, Eric Waldron, and Regina Andrews were instrumental in organizing the event and ensuring its success. Nance's contributions as a cultural bridge and advocate for African American literature and art were essential; her organizational skills and ability to foster dialogue between emerging Black writers and established figures in the literary world were pivotal in creating a seamless event that brought together diverse voices.

Regina Andrews, with her expertise as a librarian and her deep involvement in fostering Black literature, played a crucial role in promoting the careers of many writers during this period. Her meticulous planning, alongside Nance, ensured that the dinner's logistics were handled flawlessly, creating an atmosphere where creativity and collaboration could thrive. As a writer and educator, Andrews' contributions extended far beyond the dinner itself, as she continued to champion African American culture and literature throughout her career.

Eric Waldron's role as a writer and cultural organizer provided a framework for the evening's intellectual underpinnings. His efforts in promoting African American literature and supporting Black artists were critical in creating networks that uplifted their voices. Together, Johnson, Nance, Waldron, and Andrews laid the groundwork for the Harlem Renaissance's ascent.

In November 1925, Aaron Douglas arrived in New York City, having been persuaded by Ethel Ray Nance to leave Kansas City for

Harlem. His arrival marked the culmination of the Kansas City contingent: Johnson, Nance, Waldron, and now Douglas, coming together in New York. Douglas's artistic talent and unique style would be instrumental in bringing worldwide notoriety to the Harlem Renaissance. His groundbreaking works, blending African motifs with modernist aesthetics, redefined visual art and became iconic symbols of the movement's cultural and intellectual aspirations.

The evening featured a carefully curated program designed to highlight the talent and vision of the African American literary community. Charles S. Johnson's opening remarks set the tone, emphasizing the importance of creating opportunities for Black writers to share their stories with the world. His speech underscored the transformative power of literature to challenge stereotypes, foster empathy, and build bridges between communities. Langston Hughes, who was seated at a table with Ethel, Regina, and Countee Cullen at the dinner, recited "The Negro Speaks of Rivers," a poem that would later become iconic, capturing enduring strength and connection to heritage. Claude McKay also shared selections of his poetry, reflecting themes of struggle and defiance in the face of oppression. Alain Locke delivered an address previewing the themes of *The New Negro*, emphasizing the role of art and literature in redefining Black identity. Locke's words served as both inspiration and a call to action, urging attendees to continue breaking barriers and asserting their place in the cultural landscape.

The dinner's immediate impact was the validation and encouragement it provided to African American writers. For many, it was the first time their work was publicly recognized and celebrated alongside that of established literary figures. This recognition was particularly significant given the systemic barriers that Black writers faced in accessing mainstream publishing platforms. The event also strengthened networks between Black writers and white patrons, publishers, and editors. While these relationships were sometimes fraught with power imbalances, they nonetheless opened doors for African American literature to reach broader audiences. Figures like Carl Van Vechten, though controversial, played a pivotal role in connecting Black writers with influential publishers.

The Opportunity Dinner symbolized the formal emergence of the Harlem Renaissance as an organized cultural movement. It catalyzed subsequent initiatives, including the publication of Alain Locke's *The New Negro* and the expansion of platforms like *Opportunity* and *The Crisis* to amplify Black voices. For many writers in attendance, the dinner was a moment of empowerment, affirming the value of their work and emboldening them to continue challenging societal narratives and expressing the full spectrum of the Black experience.

The dinner's significance extended far beyond 1925; it marked a turning point in the Harlem Renaissance, serving as a catalyst for the movement's peak in the late 1920s and early 1930s. The writers who participated in the event would go on to produce some of the most enduring works of the era, including Langston Hughes's *The Weary Blues* and Zora Neale Hurston's *Their Eyes Were Watching God*.

Moreover, the dinner highlighted the power of intentional community building. By bringing together writers, thinkers, and patrons, Charles S. Johnson demonstrated the importance of collective action in overcoming systemic barriers. This lesson remains relevant today as artists and activists continue to navigate the challenges of representation and equity. The event also underscored the interconnectedness of art and activism. The works celebrated at the Civic Club dinner were not just artistic achievements but also acts of resistance and reclamation, challenging the dominant narratives that sought to marginalize Black voices while asserting the humanity, dignity, and creativity of African Americans.

Ethel Ray Nance's enduring impact lies in her multifaceted contributions as a writer, archivist, and advocate for justice. Her work ensured that the stories of the Harlem Renaissance were preserved and that the movement's lessons continued to inspire future generations. Regina Andrews' efforts in promoting literature and fostering community among artists solidified her as a cornerstone of the movement. Eric Waldron's dedication to creating platforms for Black voices and Aaron Douglas's transformative art became lasting symbols of the Harlem Renaissance's brilliance. Together, these individuals, alongside Charles S. Johnson, forged the connections, momentum, and confidence that launched the Harlem Renaissance into the cultural forefront.

The Opportunity Dinner at the Civic Club is rightly considered the dinner that launched the Harlem Renaissance, as it provided the platform, visibility, and unity necessary for the movement to flourish. It was a turning point that showcased the power of Black art to challenge societal norms, redefine cultural identity, and inspire change. Through their collective efforts, Nance, Johnson, Waldron, Andrews, and Douglas exemplified the resilience and brilliance that continue to define the Harlem Renaissance's legacy.

Karen Felecia Nance

Negro Writers Win Prizes

Before a magnificent gathering of writers of both races the prizes in Opportunity's Literary Contest were awarded. The prizes as awarded were as follows. The Short Story—First prize of $100 to Fog, by John Matheus, of Institute W. Va. 2nd prize $35 to Spunk, by Zora Neale Hurston of Jacksonville Fla. 3rd prize to The Voodoo's Revenge by Eric D. Waldron of New York City. For honorable mention 1 The Boll Weevil starts North by N. B. Young of St Louis Mo. 2. The Hands of Marieta Bonner. 3. Black Death by Zora Neale Hurston of Jacksonville Fla. 4. A Soul Goes West on The B. & O. by Frank Horne of Brooklyn N. Y. 5. Ante Bellum by John Davis of Lewiston Me. 6. All God's Chillun Got Shoes by N. B. Young of St Louis Mo. 7. The Examination by Eugene F. Gordon of Boston, Mass. 8. A Christmas Journey by Louis L. Redding of Atlanta Ga.

Poetry—1st prize $40 to The weary Blues by Langston Hughes Washington D. C. 2nd prize $15 To One Who Said Me Nay by Countee Cullen of New York. Third Place. For the third place there was a tie between the winners of the first and second prizes—A Song of Sour Grapes by Countee Cullen and American by Langston Hughes receiving the same number of votes. The Judges decided to award the honor to both and the cash prize to the two contestants receiving Fourth Place. Cash Prize to Solace by Clarissa Scott, Washington D. C. Cash prize of $5 to The Wayside Well by Joseph Cotter of Louisville Ky. For Honorable Mention 1. Words To My Love, by Love by Countee Cullen. 2. Symphonies by Esther Popel, of Washington D. C. 3. The Jester by Langston Hughes. 4. Songs To A Dark Virgin by Langster Hughes. 5. Preference by Dora Houston of Washington D. C. 6. My Love by Carrie McWatt of St Paul, 7. A Babe is a Babe by Joseph Cotter. 8. A Tree at Night by Helen Jehnson, 9. Brothers by Carrie W, Clifford, Washington D C, 10. Fall Of Man by Joseph Bennett, New York. 11. Lines To A Shy Woman by Robt Tard, Columbus Ohio.

Essays—1st prize of $50 to Social Equality And The Negro by E. Franklin Frazier of Atlanta Ga. 2nd prize of $30 to Roland Hayes by Sterling Brown of Lynchburg Va, 3rd prize of $10 to The Negro Poet by Laura D Wheatley of Baltimore Md.

The Press-Forum Weekly: Mobile Alabamba~Saturday, May 9, 1925

A Seat at the Table: Ethel Ray Nance & the Harlem Renaissance

Chapter 11: A Night at Dream Haven

Langston Hughes, Charles S. Johnson, E. Franklin Frazier, Rudolph Fisher, Hubert Delany, 1925

Following the groundbreaking Opportunity Dinner in 1925, the night didn't simply end. It transformed into an intimate and lively gathering at Dream Haven, the Harlem apartment shared by Ethel Ray Nance and Regina Andrews. Known as a hub for the cultural and intellectual elite of the Harlem Renaissance, Dream Haven was alive with conversation, laughter, and the aroma of sizzling bacon and eggs—a cherished staple that fueled many late-night discussions. As dawn broke over Harlem, the group ascended to the rooftop to capture a moment that would come to symbolize the collaborative energy of the era.

This iconic photograph, brimming with the vitality of the Harlem Renaissance, features five luminaries whose contributions shaped the cultural, intellectual, and social justice movements of the time: Langston Hughes, Charles S. Johnson, E. Franklin Frazier, Rudolph Fisher, and Hubert Delany.

The Luminaries in the 1925 Photograph

- **Langston Hughes**: Celebrated as the "Poet Laureate of Harlem," Hughes infused his poetry with the aspirations and struggles of Black life. Works like *The Negro Speaks of Rivers* and *I, Too,* resonated with resilience and hope. A frequent visitor to Dream Haven, Hughes found inspiration and camaraderie there, often sharing drafts and ideas. His presence in the photograph embodies his central role in the literary movement of the Renaissance.
- **Charles S. Johnson**: The visionary editor of *Opportunity: A Journal of Negro Life*, Johnson provided a platform that launched the careers of countless Black writers and artists. Beyond his editorial achievements, he orchestrated transformative events like the Civic Club Dinner, igniting the Harlem Renaissance. His collaboration with Ethel Ray Nance through Urban League initiatives showcased his unwavering commitment to social equity and cultural growth.
- **E. Franklin Frazier**: A trailblazing sociologist, Frazier's groundbreaking research illuminated the challenges facing Black communities, offering critical insights to combat systemic inequities. His shared passion for knowledge and activism with Ethel forged a bond rooted in the belief that education and advocacy were key to empowerment.
- **Rudolph Fisher**: A multifaceted talent as both a physician and writer, Fisher brought Harlem's vibrancy to life through his vivid storytelling. His literary works, rich with the sounds and textures of everyday Harlem life, captured the

Renaissance's essence. Fisher's inclusion in the photograph reflects his dual role as an observer and contributor to the cultural fabric of the time.
- **Hubert Delany**: A pioneering lawyer, judge, and civil rights advocate, Delany dedicated his career to justice and equality for African Americans. His legal work and activism echoed the broader goals of the Harlem Renaissance, and his close relationship with Ethel demonstrated the collaborative spirit that defined the movement.

This rooftop photograph from 1925, taken after a night of shared dreams and aspirations, remains a powerful testament to the enduring spirit of collaboration, creativity, and resilience that defined the Harlem Renaissance. It immortalizes a fleeting moment of unity and purpose, forever linking these visionaries to the transformative power of their time.

These photographs are more than visual records; they encapsulate the Renaissance's essence, a convergence of creativity, intellect, and advocacy. Each person in the frame represents a facet of the movement's mission to uplift and transform society. Ethel's contributions as a facilitator and advocate ensured that moments like this could happen, cementing her legacy as a driving force within the Harlem Renaissance.

Karen Felecia Nance

The Gang's All Here

Ethel Ray Nance, Langston Hughes, Helen Lanning, Pearl Fisher, Regina Andrews, Rudolph Fisher, Luella Tucker, Esther Popel Shaw, Clarissa Scott, Hubert Delany, Jessie Fauset, Mrs. Charles S. Johnson, E. Franklin Frazier.
Photo: 1925: Private collection of Karen Felecia Nance.

Ethel, Langston & Helen (1925). Private collection of Karen Felecia Nance

A Seat at the Table: Ethel Ray Nance & the Harlem Renaissance

Esther Popel, Helen Lanning, Louella Tucker, Jessie Fauset, Mrs. Charles Johnson, Ethel May Ray, Clarissa Scott Delany, Pearl Fisher (1925).
Private collection of Karen Felecia Nance

Their Contributions to the Harlem Renaissance

Ethel Ray Nance played a pivotal role as assistant to Charles S. Johnson, editor of *Opportunity: A Journal of Negro Life*, and one of the leading architects of the Harlem Renaissance. Her organizational expertise and connections facilitated cultural events, such as the historic 1924 Civic Club Dinner, which launched the Renaissance as a cohesive movement. Through her role, Ethel supported emerging artists, fostered collaboration, and provided a vital link between Harlem's intellectual and artistic communities.

Langston Hughes, often referred to as the "Poet Laureate of Harlem," was a foundational figure in the Harlem Renaissance. His poetry, including works like "The Weary Blues" and "Mother to Son," celebrated Black culture and resilience while addressing themes of racial identity and social justice. Hughes was a frequent visitor to Dream Haven, where his readings and exchanges with other creatives were instrumental in shaping the cultural narrative of the era.

Helen Lanning, the sister of Jessie Fauset, contributed to the Harlem Renaissance through her intellectual influence and support of the artistic community. Though not as widely recognized, Lanning's presence reflected the interconnectedness of families and networks that bolstered the movement. Her connections to key figures in literature and art further underscored her importance.

Pearl Fisher added vibrancy to the Renaissance as a patron and supporter of its cultural endeavors. While specific details about her contributions are less documented, her involvement in the community highlighted the critical role of individuals who fostered the development of creative spaces.

Regina Andrews, a librarian at the 135th Street Library, was a central figure in connecting Harlem's artists and intellectuals. Her library became a meeting place for discussions on race, culture, and art, and her home at Dream Haven served as a sanctuary for luminaries such as Langston Hughes and Zora Neale Hurston. Andrews' commitment to education and community engagement made her a cornerstone of the Renaissance.

Rudolph Fisher was a physician, writer, and musician whose literary works vividly captured Harlem life. His stories, including "The City of Refuge," explored themes of migration and identity, offering nuanced portrayals of the Black experience. As a regular attendee of Dream Haven gatherings, Fisher's contributions enriched the intellectual and creative dialogues of the period.

A Seat at the Table: Ethel Ray Nance & the Harlem Renaissance

Luella Tucker, who worked in the *Opportunity* office, was instrumental in organizing and supporting the magazine's operations. Her involvement ensured the publication's ability to spotlight emerging Black talent, making *Opportunity* a cornerstone of the Harlem Renaissance.

Esther Popel Shaw was a poet whose work celebrated African American identity and challenged racial injustice. Her poetry, published in key magazines like *Opportunity*, contributed to the literary richness of the Harlem Renaissance. Shaw's voice added depth to the movement's exploration of race and culture.

Clarissa Scott, a poet and intellectual, offered a fresh perspective through her writings, which often explored themes of identity, womanhood, and social justice. Her contributions to the Harlem Renaissance highlighted the intersection of gender and race, adding complexity to the movement's discourse.

Hubert Delany was a lawyer, judge, and civil rights advocate whose work extended the Renaissance's influence into legal and social reform. Delany's efforts to combat racial discrimination and promote justice complemented the cultural strides of the movement, reinforcing its broader mission of equality.

Jessie Fauset, a poet, novelist, and editor at *The Crisis*, was one of the most influential literary figures of the Harlem Renaissance. Her novels, such as *Plum Bun*, explored themes of racial passing and identity, while her editorial work provided a platform for emerging Black writers, including Langston Hughes. Fauset's mentorship and literary contributions were instrumental in shaping the Renaissance's legacy.

Mrs. Charles Johnson, though often in the background, played a vital role in hosting gatherings and fostering an environment of support for artists and intellectuals. Her hospitality and partnership with Charles S. Johnson created opportunities for collaboration and dialogue among Harlem's cultural leaders.

E. Franklin Frazier, a sociologist, offered critical insights into the social structure of Black communities. His research highlighted systemic inequities and informed the Renaissance's broader mission of advocating social justice. Frazier's scholarly contributions provided a framework for understanding the societal challenges that the movement sought to address.

Together, these figures embodied the spirit of the Harlem Renaissance, a dynamic interplay of art, intellect, and activism. Everyone's contributions enriched the movement, leaving a legacy that continues to inspire cultural and social progress.

Preservation of the Photographs

The photographs, which have been displayed in exhibitions and circulated widely, serve as enduring reminders of the Renaissance's cultural impact. While Ethel was proud of the moments they captured, she was also protective of their significance. When Regina Andrews allowed the photograph of Hughes, Johnson, Frazier, Fisher, and Delany to be used in a Metropolitan Museum of Art exhibition, Ethel was initially thrilled. However, her excitement turned to frustration when she discovered the image had been reproduced on postcards for sale, an act she felt commodified a deeply personal memory. For Ethel, these photographs were not just mementos but symbols of the spirit of Harlem in the 1920s spirit she helped nurture and one that continues to inspire generations.

The New York Public Library Digital Collections has 20 personal photographs listed under the Regina Andrews photograph collection; these two photographs, along with others, were housed with Ethel Ray Nance and are now in the private collection of Karen Felecia Nance. https://digitalcollections.nypl.org/collections/regina-andrews-photograph-collection#/?tab=navigation

Today, The Edge Harlem restaurant stands as a bridge between past and present. Located in the same building where Ethel once lived with Regina and Louella, the restaurant honors her legacy and the creative energy of the Renaissance. These 1925 images displayed here invite reflection on the transformative power of community, collaboration, and the courage to reimagine a future shaped by justice, resilience, and collective progress.

Together, these figures embodied the spirit of the Harlem Renaissance, a dynamic interplay of art, intellect, and activism. Everyone's contributions enriched the movement, leaving a legacy that continues to inspire cultural and social progress.

Chapter 12: Luminaries and Legacy: Shaping the Harlem Renaissance

Ethel Ray Nance and Harlem's Luminaries: A Tapestry of Influence and Connection

Ethel Ray Nance's life was deeply intertwined with the Harlem Renaissance, an era of cultural luminaries like W.E.B. Du Bois, Langston Hughes, Zora Neale Hurston, Regina Anderson Andrews, Aaron Douglas, and others highlight the interconnectedness of a movement that shaped American culture and beyond. Each figure brought a unique vision to the Renaissance, enriching its legacy and inspiring future generations. Here, their contributions and connections to Ethel are explored in depth.

Ethel's personal stories about these luminaries offer a glimpse into the collaborative and vibrant world of the Harlem Renaissance. These anecdotes, filled with humor, warmth, and respect, not only humanize the figures we now revere but also highlight the interconnectedness of a movement that reshaped American culture.

Charles S. Johnson: Mapping the Black Experience

Charles S. Johnson was a towering figure in the Harlem Renaissance, shaping its cultural and intellectual trajectory through his work with the National Urban League and as editor of *Opportunity: A Journal of Negro Life.* As the league's director of research and publicity, Johnson focused on addressing systemic inequalities and improving the social and economic conditions of African Americans. Under his leadership, the National Urban

League became a key institution in promoting racial uplift, providing resources, and fostering Black cultural expression during the Renaissance.

Johnson's role as editor of *Opportunity* was particularly transformative. The magazine became a vital platform for Black writers, artists, and thinkers, providing them with a space to share their work and ideas. *Opportunity* played a central role in showcasing the talents of luminaries such as Langston Hughes, Zora Neale Hurston, and Countee Cullen. Johnson not only published their works but also created opportunities for collaboration and recognition by organizing contests and events that celebrated emerging Black talent. Notably, the 1925 Civic Club Dinner, orchestrated by Johnson, brought together Black creatives and influential white patrons, formally launching the Harlem Renaissance and cementing its cultural significance.

Ethel Ray Nance worked closely with Johnson as his assistant, contributing to his efforts at the National Urban League and *Opportunity* magazine. Her responsibilities included research, proofreading, and organizing events and contests that highlighted Black excellence. Ethel recalled how Johnson's mentorship challenged her to grow:

"I never felt better than I did as a young person, being away from home and all. I really felt that anything could be accomplished there in New York. You felt—I had to do a lot of research for Charles Johnson, and he gave me long assignments and tough assignments and he never explained anything, and he expected me to work it out. But it was wonderful training. I had to do all the proofreading for

the Opportunity magazine." (Interview with David Taylor, May 25, 1974, page 36)

Through these experiences, Ethel honed her skills and became deeply embedded in the cultural and intellectual currents of the Renaissance.

A Seat at the Table: Ethel Ray Nance & the Harlem Renaissance

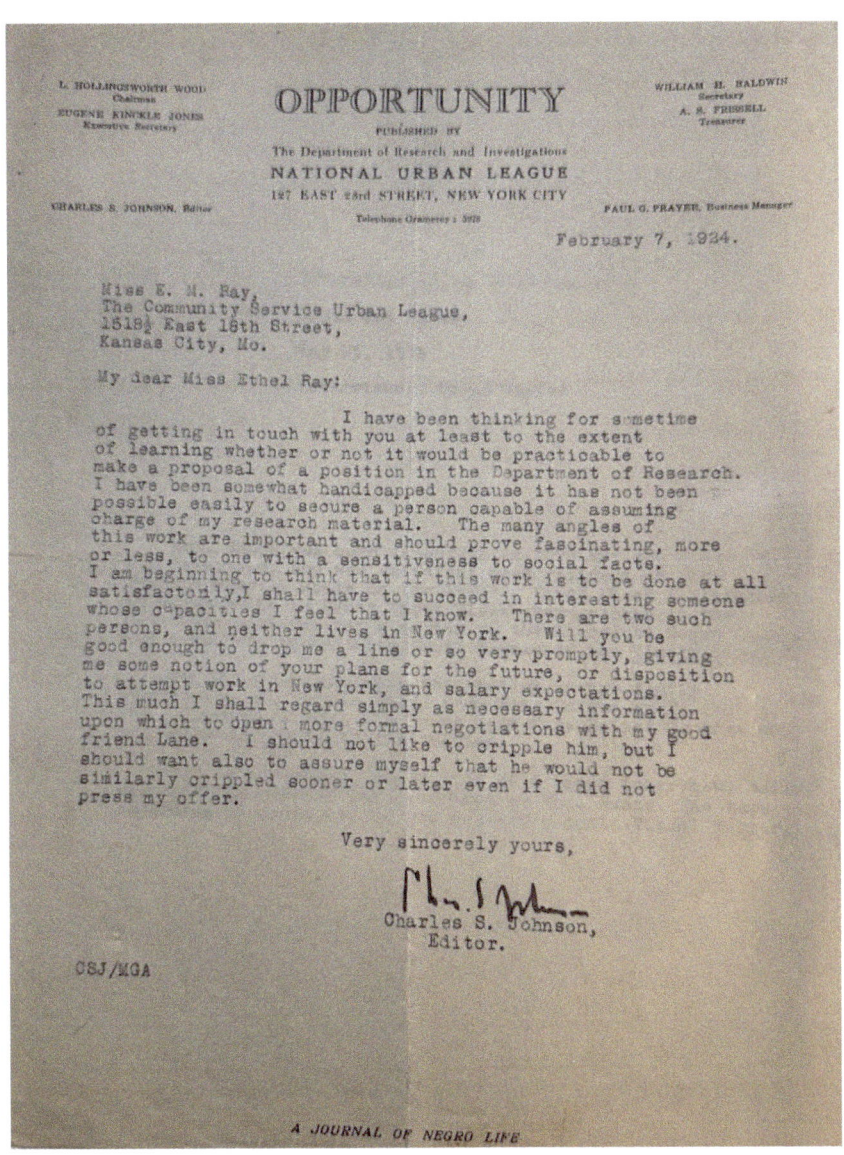

Letter from Charles S. Johnson to E. M. Ray dated 2/7/1924. Private collection of Karen Felecia Nance

Johnson's influence extended far beyond the pages of *Opportunity*. His sociological research illuminated systemic inequalities, and his ability to connect artists, writers, and intellectuals fostered a sense of unity and shared purpose within the movement. Ethel's work alongside him not only supported his ambitious projects but also gave her a front-row seat to the Harlem Renaissance's transformative power. Together, they contributed to an era that redefined African American identity, promoted cultural pride, and challenged the status quo through art and intellect.

By assisting Johnson in his multifaceted roles, Ethel played an integral part in the success of his initiatives, helping to amplify the voices of Black artists and thinkers. Their collaboration reflects the collective effort and determination that defined the Harlem Renaissance, a period that continues to inspire and shape American culture.

Ethel was upset that everyone was getting credit except Charles S. Johnson.

"I was very upset because everybody was getting credit for helping the young writers except Charles Johnson. They were giving a great deal of credit to Carl Van Vechten and that provoked me. Alain Locke should have had credit; he was also one of our judges. He should have had credit because he was very important to the movement."

(Ethel Ray Nance's interview with David Taylor, May 25, 1974, page 32.)

A Seat at the Table: Ethel Ray Nance & the Harlem Renaissance

She expressed her concerns to the Johnson Publishing Company, Inc., in a letter dated March 10, 1972, specifically addressing the omission of Charles S. Johnson in the company's books about the Harlem Renaissance period.

Ethel referred to her 1968 article in a letter to Johnson publishing company dated March 10, 1972:

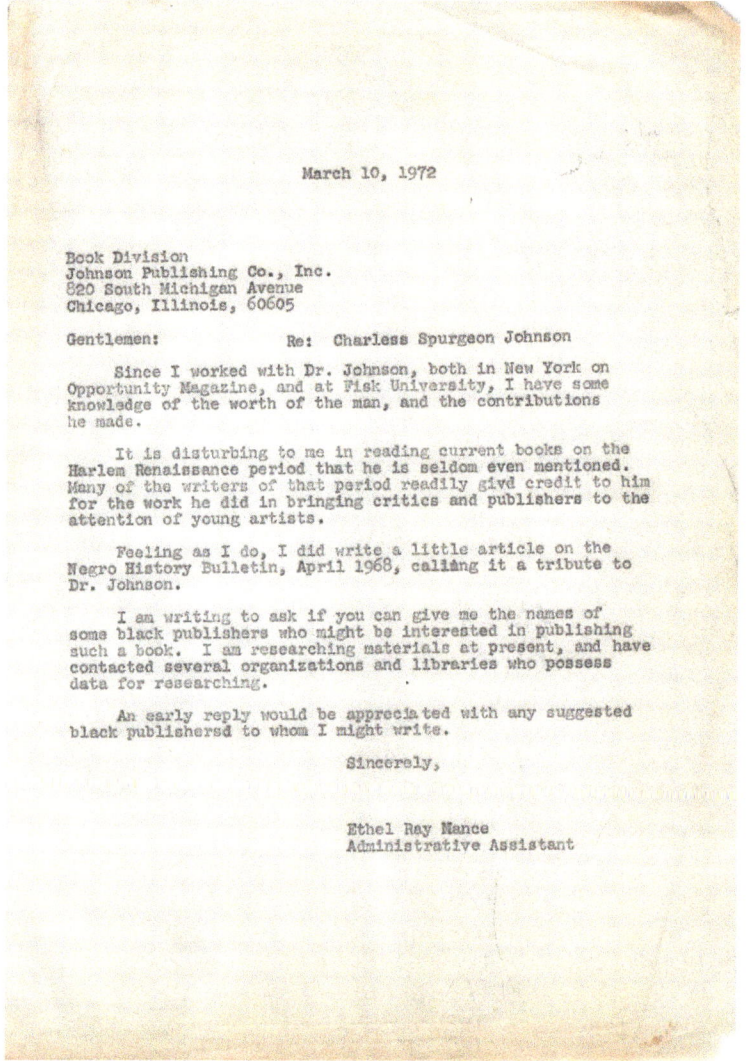

March 10, 1972 letter from Ethel Ray Nance to Johnson Publishing Private collection of Karen Felecia Nance

The article, *The New York Arts Renaissance 1924–26,"* published in the *Negro History Bulletin* in April 1968, offers an insightful firsthand account of the Harlem Renaissance during its peak years. Drawing from her personal experiences as a participant in this cultural movement, Ethel highlights the flourishing of African American arts and culture during this transformative period. She emphasizes the emergence of new cultural expressions across various art forms, including literature, music, visual arts, and theater, and underscores the importance of these works in challenging racial stereotypes, promoting Black identity, and fostering a sense of pride within the African American community.

Ethel's article discusses how this artistic movement not only provided a platform for Black artists but also engaged with broader social and political issues, reflecting the struggles and aspirations of the African American community. She highlights key figures who were instrumental in shaping the period's vibrancy, as well as the significance of institutions and organizations that supported these artists. Moreover, she examines the impact of cultural exchanges within and beyond the Harlem community, illustrating how this collaborative spirit enriched the movement's creativity and influence.

Through her narrative, Ethel conveys the profound influence of the Harlem Renaissance on American culture and its enduring legacy. She reflects on the vibrant artistic and intellectual activities that defined Harlem between 1924 and 1926, providing valuable insights into the challenges and triumphs faced by African American artists. Her work illustrates how this cultural renaissance shaped a pivotal era in history and continues to inspire generations.

Nance, Ethel Ray. "THE NEW YORK ARTS RENAISSANCE 1924-1926." *Negro History Bulletin*, vol. 31, no. 4, 1968, pp. 15–19.

W.E.B. Du Bois: The Strategist of Social Change

This chapter celebrates the whimsy of Marielle and André while also delving into the rich tapestry of friendships and collaborations that defined Ethel's life in Harlem. It reminds us that history is not just shaped by grand events but also by the intimate, everyday interactions that fuel creativity and connection.

W.E.B. Du Bois, a towering intellectual and co-founder of the NAACP, played a pivotal role in advancing the social and cultural aspirations of Black Americans. Through his editorship of *The Crisis* magazine, Du Bois provided a platform for emerging Black writers, poets, and artists, fostering the creative explosion of the Harlem Renaissance. His disciplined, methodical approach to work inspired many, including Ethel.

Ethel and Du Bois shared a professional and personal bond spanning over four decades. She worked closely with him during the founding of the United Nations in San Francisco in 1945, assisting him in drafting proposals on colonial issues. Ethel's organizational skills complemented Du Bois's vision, and her recollections of his humor and kindness added depth to his otherwise austere public persona. Du Bois frequently visited Ethel's family during his travels, and their collaborations underscored her significant role in shaping his projects.

Just about everyone who knew Ethel wanted to meet Du Bois. Occasionally, he would attend one of their gatherings. When he did, it was a notable occasion, as he typically had little time for such events. Generally, he would not remain for long. However, on certain occasions, when he sought respite from his demanding schedule, he would take Ethel and her roommates out to dinner or treat them to lunch in Greenwich Village, often choosing hot dogs, and he would permit each of them one glass of beer. Ethel, Regina, and Louella were only paid once a month. Their salaries were not large, and they paid $85 a month in rent, which was a great deal. So toward the end of the month, usually the last week, they would call DuBois and ask him how he was. If he was in town, he would say, "I presume you're hungry." Then, he would take them out to dinner. He was very nice about that. Ethel expressed that he was very nice about it and he got "quite a kick" out of them.

Through her secretarial and administrative work with W.E.B. DuBois and Charles S. Johnson, Ethel made significant contributions to the Harlem Renaissance and became instrumental in its reconstruction in later years.

Du Bois and Johnson exclusively entrusted Ethel with their research, scheduling, and event planning, refusing to allow anyone else to fulfill these roles due to her exceptional talent.

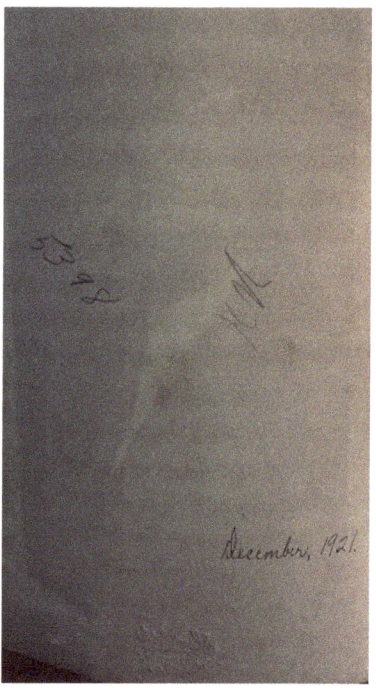

Inscription: W.E.B. DuBois to Ethel May Ray ~Back of Photo is dated: December 1921

Regina Anderson Andrews: The Cultural Gatekeeper

Regina Anderson Andrews, a librarian at the 135th Street Library, was a linchpin in Harlem's literary and artistic community. Her library served as a hub for intellectual exchange, while her shared apartment with Ethel, known as *Dream Haven*, became a gathering place for luminaries like Langston Hughes, Aaron Douglas, and Zora Neale Hurston. Regina's work with *Opportunity* magazine and her commitment to uplifting Black voices made her a vital figure in the Renaissance.

Ethel's partnership with Regina exemplified the power of collaboration. Together, they organized the *Opportunity* Dinner, which formally launched the Renaissance by celebrating emerging Black talent. Regina's refined intellect and Ethel's practical support created a dynamic synergy that enriched Harlem's cultural fabric. Ethel met Regina on June 16, 1924, at an impromptu party at 102 Edgecombe, marking the beginning of a lifelong bond rooted in mutual admiration, complementary strengths, and a shared commitment to fostering creativity and social progress.

Regina, whom Ethel affectionately described as a "lifesaver," was a key connector in Harlem's arts community through her role as a librarian. She connected students and publishers and wrote while dedicating herself to reviewing and summarizing stacks of books, showcasing her tireless commitment to knowledge and creativity. Ethel admired Regina's intellectual rigor and grace, awed by her ability to connect with and support leading figures of the time.

Together, Ethel Ray Nance and Regina Anderson Andrews transformed *Dream Haven*, their apartment, which they shared with Louella Tucker at 580 St. Nicholas Avenue, into a sanctuary for creativity and collaboration. As detailed in Ethelene Whitmire's biography, *Regina Anderson Andrews: Harlem Renaissance Librarian, Dream Haven* fostered an environment where intellectual exchange thrived, making it a cornerstone of the Harlem Renaissance. Regina was a delicate and graceful presence, a woman of striking beauty and refined charm. She was a Chicago-born intellectual with roots in Wisconsin, the daughter of an attorney who incentivized her to keep her hair long, a choice that set her apart during the "bobbed hair" trend of the 1920s. Styling her hair high on her head in a Spanish fashion, she added to her timeless allure, which complemented her refined demeanor and intellectual prowess. A. Philip Randolph's decision to feature her on the December 1924 cover of *The Messenger* was not only a testament to her beauty but also a reflection of her cultural significance and the role she played in shaping the Harlem Renaissance.

A Seat at the Table: Ethel Ray Nance & the Harlem Renaissance

https://www.marxists.org/history/usa/pubs/messenger/v6n12-dec-1924-Messenger-riaz-cov.pdf

Dream Haven stood as more than just an apartment—it was a hub of innovation, dialogue, and inspiration. The collaborative atmosphere nurtured by Ethel, Regina, and Louella helped bridge the worlds of art, literature, and activism, solidifying its place as a symbol of the Renaissance's dynamic energy.

Ethel also formed a close friendship with Regina's husband, William T. Andrews, a prominent attorney and civil rights advocate. Andrews played a significant role in the Harlem Renaissance by using his legal expertise to fight for racial justice and equality. He was instrumental in providing legal counsel for cases involving civil rights violations and worked tirelessly to dismantle systemic barriers facing the Black community. Andrews was a member of the NAACP and a staunch advocate for education, believing that intellectual empowerment was a key avenue for racial uplift. His unwavering commitment to justice and his contributions to the movement made him a respected figure in Harlem's activist and intellectual circles.

The Andrews household exemplified the Renaissance's spirit of collaboration, blending art, activism, and intellectual pursuits. Ethel admired William's dedication to justice, recognizing how his legal work complemented Regina's cultural endeavors. Together, the couple embodied a partnership that bridged the realms of advocacy and creativity, and Ethel's friendship with both of them enriched her understanding of the interconnectedness of these pursuits.

Whitmire underscores Ethel and Regina's instrumental role in organizing the Opportunity Dinner. Their meticulous planning and extensive networks were crucial to the event's success, which showcased Black talent and cemented the cultural impact of the Harlem Renaissance. Regina's literary expertise and social charm complemented Ethel's grounded pragmatism, creating a partnership that reflected the Renaissance's collaborative spirit.

Ethel's impact extended far beyond *Dream Haven.* She co-edited the *Chronology of the African Americans in New York City and Environs from 1621 to 1966* with Regina and James H. Smith, preserving the legacy of African American contributions in New York. In addition to her editorial work, Ethel's role as an assistant to Charles S. Johnson, editor of *Opportunity,* allowed her to advance the careers of Black artists and writers. She conducted research, organized events, and facilitated introductions that elevated voices often overlooked by mainstream institutions. Ethel's support was instrumental in fostering the Renaissance's inclusive and transformative environment.

While the Harlem Renaissance is often celebrated for its prolific writers and artists, Ethel's contributions as a facilitator, editor, and advocate were equally vital. Her partnership with Regina Anderson Andrews and her friendship with William T. Andrews exemplified how collaboration and shared purpose could amplify the brilliance of others. Together, they created spaces and opportunities that profoundly shaped the cultural landscape of their time.

Ethel's reflections on Regina and William brimmed with gratitude and admiration. She often marveled at how much she learned from their shared experiences, recognizing that their partnerships expanded her understanding of culture, society, and justice. Through their enduring friendship, the creation of *Dream*

Haven, and their role in organizing transformative events like the Opportunity Dinner, Ethel Ray Nance, Regina Anderson Andrews, and William T. Andrews left an indelible mark on the Harlem Renaissance. Their vision, resilience, and commitment to fostering brilliance in others ensured that the voices of Black creatives were not only heard but preserved for future generations.

William (Bill) and Regina Andrews,1972. Private collection of Karen Felecia Nance

Ethel, in contrast, saw herself as a Midwestern "corn-fed country gal," humble yet deeply aware of her evolving place in this dynamic world. Yet, Ethel's physical strength and practicality complemented Regina's delicate demeanor. Whether it was moving heavy furniture, offering steadfast support, or engaging in meaningful discussions, Ethel brought a grounded pragmatism that balanced Regina's refinement.

Jessie Fauset, Regina Anderson Andrews, Ethel Ray Nance, Photo taken abt 1927. Private collection of Karen Felecia Nance

Their dynamic highlighted how their differences made their partnership stronger. Regina's literary expertise and social charm brought cultural depth to their shared endeavors, while Ethel contributed her enthusiasm, reliability, and warmth. Together, they created not just a home but a haven for the intellectual and artistic titans of their time. Ethel often reflected on how much she learned from Regina and their shared experiences, marveling at the opportunities this sisterhood provided to expand her world and deepen her understanding of culture and society.

Whitmire's biography sheds light on the enduring personal bond between Regina and Ethel, a friendship rooted in mutual respect and shared aspirations that spanned decades. This deep connection extended far beyond their professional collaborations, forming a bedrock of support and companionship throughout their lives.

Ethel was not only a host but an active collaborator. She co-edited the *Chronology of African-Americans in New York, 1621-1966,* with Regina Anderson Andrews, providing a critical historical record of the Black experience in New York. Her editorial contributions helped document and preserve the era's rich legacy. Additionally, Nance's work extended beyond literary pursuits. As an assistant to Charles S. Johnson, a prominent sociologist, and editor of *Opportunity* magazine, she played a role in advancing the careers of numerous Black artists and writers by facilitating introductions and promoting their works. Her impact on the Harlem Renaissance went beyond the confines of her apartment and editorial projects. Her dedication to documenting and amplifying Black voices underscored her belief in the transformative power of literature and art to foster social change. While the Renaissance is often celebrated for its prolific writers, Nance's contributions as a behind-the-scenes facilitator, editor, and advocate were equally vital in ensuring that the voices of Black creatives were heard and preserved for future generations.

Through her collaboration with Andrews and her deep commitment to cultural preservation, Ethel Ray Nance remains an unsung hero of the Harlem Renaissance, a testament to the indispensable role of those who worked tirelessly to amplify the voices of others.

A Seat at the Table: Ethel Ray Nance & the Harlem Renaissance

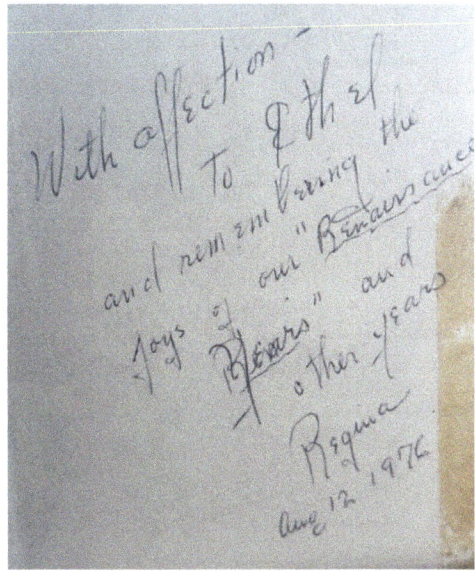

Left: Front photo of Regina Anderson. **Right:** Back of Photo's inscription: With affection to Ethel and remembering the joys of our "Renaissance Years" and other years. Regina, dated August 12, 1976

Fauset Redmon Fauset: The Literary Architect of Harlem's Literary Renaissance

Jessie Fauset was a pivotal figure in the Harlem Renaissance, a movement that celebrated African American culture and artistic expression in the early 20th century. As a writer, editor, and intellectual, Fauset made significant contributions to literature and the arts, shaping the narrative that defined the era. Her relationship with fellow writers, including Ethel Ray Nance, further illustrates her role as a connector and champion of Black artists and writers during this transformative period.

Born on April 27, 1882, in Camden, New Jersey, Jessie Fauset was the daughter of an African Methodist Episcopal Church minister. Her upbringing instilled in her a strong sense of identity and the importance of education. Fauset attended the prestigious Philadelphia High School for Girls and later graduated from Cornell University in 1905, becoming the first African American woman to earn a degree in classical languages. Her education and background provided her with a unique perspective on race, culture, and identity. These experiences would later influence her literary works, where she skillfully combined traditional narrative techniques with contemporary themes to explore the complexities of African American life.

Fauset's role as literary editor of *The Crisis,* the official magazine of the NAACP, was instrumental in shaping the literary landscape of the Harlem Renaissance. Her editorial leadership from 1919 to 1926 helped establish *The Crisis* as a platform for emerging Black writers, offering them a venue to refine their voices. She played a crucial role in promoting the careers of literary figures such as Langston Hughes, Zora Neale Hurston, and Claude McKay, ensuring that their works reached broader audiences.

Ethel Ray Nance recalled her admiration for Faucet's role in *The Crisis*, noting how closely she worked with Dr. W.E.B. Du Bois: *"She was very, very helpful on The Crisis magazine and admired Dr. Du Bois very much. She had been a teacher before she started working for him, and her skillfulness in languages and extensive travels abroad made her invaluable."* Fauset's literary achievements, including her first novel, *There is Confusion* (1924), were celebrated at key events like the first literary contest dinner, where she became a central figure of the Renaissance.

Ethel first encountered Fauset at a luncheon at the Civic Club in Greenwich Village, a private venue that required a member to invite guests. She recalled being startled upon seeing Fauset smoking, as it clashed with the decorum she associated with Du Bois's circle. Reflecting on this moment, Ethel said: *"It isn't that I hadn't seen women smoke before, but it seemed that anyone associated with Dr. Du Bois—there was a certain position there, and I think it startled me at first. But she was very graceful at it."* Fauset later joked, *"Men don't give me candy; they give me cigarettes,"* showcasing her wit and individuality. Ethel remembered Fauset's collection of cigarettes, including the vibrant *Salomes,* which came in colored wrappers matching evening gowns—a testament to her elegance and attention to detail.

https://kyhistory.pastperfectonline.com/webobject/8B00ED0D-7C0A-4D78-BF6B-956311535875

A Seat at the Table: Ethel Ray Nance & the Harlem Renaissance

Ethel recorded in her diary her lunch at the Civic Club on August 6, 1924:

> Diary
> Aug. 6, 1924
>
> Am lunching at the Civic Club today on 12th Street near 5th Avenue. "For members only" then how come I? Well, Dr. DuBois was kind enough to secure a guest card for me which admits me during the month of August. They serve only at noon.
>
> This was a former residence. You enter a hall which seems spacious because of the small over-all space. On the left side is the general office, then the checkroom where you register and leave your wraps, buy your ticket for lunch. Continuting to your right down a narrow hallway you descend 5 or 6 steps and find yourself in the dining room, plainly furnished but with an intimate Bohemian atmosphere. Tables for 2 and 4 are lined on each side of the room with a large long oval family table in the center which could accommodate around 20. At each end of the room are round dining room tables. The club is very simply furnished. The walls are brick, painted buff color down to within 3 feet of the floor where a 3-inch border of red separates the lower portion which is painted burnt orange. The tables are neat with fresh white linen, and the chairs are a pretty green.
>
> Dr. DuBois and Miss Jessie Fauset are seated at the next table. I have ordered, and am scribbling notes to send home. They ask me to join them. I had met Miss Fauset before at the Crisis office and found her very friendly. She is beautiful, gracious and I hope I didn't just stare at her as she talked. I had never met anyone like her before. She was talking about a proposed trip to France, and from the conversation she would contact some mutual friends of theirs, with specific duties to perform for Dr. DuBois. How wonderful it was for me, to be close to people who traveled around the world and could speak of it just as casually as I might in contemplating a trip to Chicago. One thing disturbed me. Both of them were smoking cigarettes.

While I had seen many women smoke at the Club on previous visits, still I had never known one. Somehow it seemed to put her out of character, in spite of the fact she managed to be very graceful -- she seemed to be the type you would expect to be against such a past time.

Later when we became better acquainted she showed me two or three different varieties in her desk drawer at the office, smiling, and said " Men never give me candy - they always give cigarettes!" It was the first time I had ever seen Salomes - cigarette with wrappers in different colors. "To match your gown," she said.

Oh yes, back to the Club - there is one window and a sky-light forming a triangle in the corner. In the evening I'm sure the effect would be pleasing. Two chandeliers hang from the ceiling by chains - the fixtures are upright resembling candle holders (6 of them on each chain), topped with orange parchment shades that are finished off with a narrow band of black at top and bottom.

A Seat at the Table: Ethel Ray Nance & the Harlem Renaissance

(I am very grateful that my parents kept letters I had written home so that some incidents could be pinpointed during these years.)

The daughter, Yolanda, was away at school. I found Mrs. DuBois very friendly in a quiet, retiring way. Dr. DuBois inquired why I hadn;t written the Crisis if I wished to come to New York instead of "coming to work for a"rival" magazine! In a mock serious tone he added, "I'm surprised that your father permitted it!" I explained that I had come directly from mu job in Kansas City and that my father was not aware of my decision.

"Anyhow," I added, "I had not received an offer from the Crisis!"

Diary

Feb. 14, 1924 - Dr. DuBois took me to dinner at the Civic Club, and I told him about your congratulatory comments on the February Crisis. He was pleased and asked me to thank you.

June 28, 1925 - Marvel Jackson (whose home is in Minneapolis) is doing Spanish translations in Washington for the government. (She is supposed to look enough like me to be my twin.) will be visiting us over the 4th of July. Dr. DuBois will be back in town next week. I hope he comes in time so she can meet him.

Ethel's diary entry: August 6, 1924. Private collection of Karen Felecia Nance

Ethel's own relationship with Du Bois is colored by humor and mutual respect. Having moved to New York to work for *Opportunity* magazine under Charles S. Johnson, she found herself frequently teased by Du Bois, who would say, *"You came to New York to work for... uh... a rival magazine!"* Ethel's playful response, *"Well, I wasn't offered a job with The Crisis,"* reflected both her wit and her deep admiration for his work. This exchange highlights the dynamic interplay of competition and camaraderie that characterized the relationships among the era's intellectuals and writers.

Fauset's influence extended beyond her editorial work. Her novels explored themes of racial identity, gender dynamics, and class struggles with a level of sophistication that resonated deeply with her contemporaries. Ethel described her as *"not by any means one of the lesser writers of that period."* Works like *Plum Bun* (1928) tackled the challenges of passing and identity, while *The Chinaberry Tree* (1931) and *Comedy: American Style* (1933) delved into the aspirations and struggles of Black middle-class families.

Beyond her writing, Fauset's Sunday afternoon teas became a cherished tradition within the Harlem Renaissance. Ethel recalled: *"It was common practice between certain hours that you would drop by Faucet's. And there you would meet interesting people. You could bring anyone you wanted, but there was a certain decorum when you entered her house. Fauset just reflected that."* These gatherings were informal yet intellectual, fostering connections among artists, writers, and thinkers. They were quintessentially Fauset—graceful, welcoming, and imbued with an air of sophistication.

A Seat at the Table: Ethel Ray Nance & the Harlem Renaissance

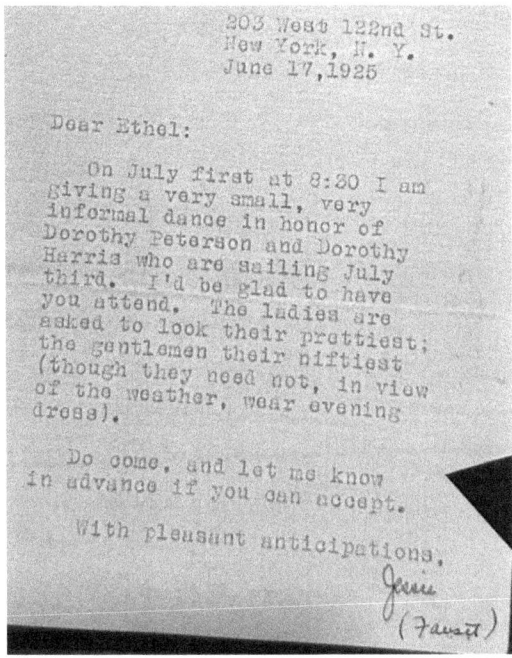

Fauset's invitation to Ethel for tea. June 17, 1925

Ethel shared fond memories of Fauset's generosity and elegance. On one occasion, Fauset admired a dress Ethel was wearing and suggested they exchange outfits. Ethel, hesitant to accept what she described as a *"Parisian gown"* in exchange for her own modest dress, declined, reflecting on how Fauset's worldly sophistication added an intangible value to even the simplest items.

Fauset's life also revealed her adaptability and resilience. She married late in life, reportedly to a teacher, and eventually returned to her roots in education. Despite societal shifts, Ethel doubted that Fauset would have adjusted to the evolving language and cultural norms of later decades, observing: *"She wasn't a person that would probably fit in today at all. She would have been against this new language which we've acquired."* Yet, Fauset's timeless qualities—her intellect, elegance, and dedication—remained what mattered most to Ethel, who concluded, *"What does age matter anyhow? She was a beautiful person."*

Ethel's relationship with Fauset exemplified the collaborative spirit of the Harlem Renaissance, where individuals worked together to elevate African American voices and culture. Ethel recalled her integration into the world of Fauset and Dr. Du Bois, noting: *"Dr. Du Bois knew my father, and I was accepted into the family!"* While Ethel worked for *Opportunity,* the rival magazine to *The Crisis,* their shared mission to foster creativity and progress transcended any sense of competition.

Jessie Fauset's legacy as a writer, editor, and mentor endures as a cornerstone of the Harlem Renaissance. Through her relationship with Ethel Ray Nance, the collaborative and interconnected nature of the Renaissance is vividly illustrated. Together, they and their peers created a cultural movement that reshaped the narrative of African American identity and paved the way for future generations.

A Seat at the Table: Ethel Ray Nance & the Harlem Renaissance

Ethel's June 29, 1925, letter to her parents discusses the New York events, including Jessie Fauset's teas. *(Private collection of Karen Felecia Nance)*

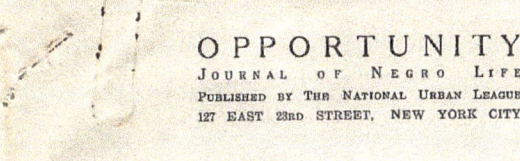

Marvel Kay Jackson and Ethel: July 4th, 1925, Staten Island, New York. Private collection of Karen Felecia Nance.

OPPORTUNITY
JOURNAL OF NEGRO LIFE
PUBLISHED BY THE NATIONAL URBAN LEAGUE
127 EAST 23RD STREET, NEW YORK CITY

OFFICE OF
CHARLES S. JOHNSON
    EDITOR   –2–

    Miss Fauset has a little party on Wednesday evening for 2 girls who leave for Europe next week to be gone for the summer. Last week Regina, Luella and I went down to see a Washington school teacher off. No, you didn't meet her – this girl has been given a scholarship to study art in Paris for a year and a half. Her boat left at 12:30 at night. Many people leave at night now – it seems that puts them in France in the morning and is preferred.

    Both of the Washington girls, Bertha McNeil and Esther Popel, told me they heard from you. Regina and Luelle also heard from you last week.

OPPORTUNITY
JOURNAL OF NEGRO LIFE
PUBLISHED BY THE NATIONAL URBAN LEAGUE
127 EAST 23RD STREET, NEW YORK CITY

OFFICE OF
CHARLES S. JOHNSON
EDITOR

-3-

Glad to hear Mrs. Asbjornsen called. Hope Nina is well. Hello to Mrs. Forsgren when you happen to see her. I have dropped them all cards from time to time.

Dr. DuBois will be back next week. I hope he comes in time so I may have Marvel meet him and possibly he'll take us to lunch at the Civic Club - he's lovely about that.

Dorothy Steele's mother and daughter are coming next week some time to spend a few months with her. She is very happy preparing for them.

Must go,

Ethel

OPPORTUNITY
JOURNAL OF NEGRO LIFE
PUBLISHED BY THE NATIONAL URBAN LEAGUE
127 EAST 23RD STREET, NEW YORK CITY

—4—

OFFICE OF
CHARLES S. JOHNSON
EDITOR

I notice your comments on "Spunk." Portraying life as it is is an art. We didn't care for Dunbar because he did. We thought he was holding up our shortcomings for everyone to see. We all have shortcomings and to deny them or to refuse to acknowledge them is an exhibition of weakness rather than strength. To portray life as it is, is art. It somewhat surprises me that you shouldn't like this because you don't seem to have any qualms of conscience about picturing life as it is from your accounts of the South with its poverty of life and living / up to comments on your work and associates in Duluth. We know these things exist, just as other people know they exist. For us to pass over them makes the other person

OPPORTUNITY
JOURNAL OF NEGRO LIFE
PUBLISHED BY THE NATIONAL URBAN LEAGUE
127 EAST 23RD STREET, NEW YORK CITY

-5-

OFFICE OF
CHARLES S. JOHNSON
EDITOR

who knows this is life, and who knows that we know this is life, wonder what we feel so sensitive about - the truth does make us wince now and then, but simply because we awake suddenly to the fact that what we already knew others knew too. And that after all life is life. I should think you would like the way the story is worked out if one is to continue in your points of criticism because retribution surely shows up by the aid of superstition, or the ghost of the dead man. Most of the judges in commenting on the story mentioned Zora's strong use of words, how she painted pictures strongly - her style was compared to that of a man's, rather brutal and direct.

OPPORTUNITY
JOURNAL OF NEGRO LIFE
PUBLISHED BY THE NATIONAL URBAN LEAGUE
127 EAST 23RD STREET, NEW YORK CITY

OFFICE OF
CHARLES S. JOHNSON
EDITOR

It's very convenient to dispose of people who don't fit into our schemes by murder, that's why some times I wonder why people waste so much *time and energy* going to God to ask him to forgive people their sins. It's much simpler when we feel we have a God-given power of knowing right and wrong, when we feel that we have the right to judge, to simply carry out our judgment. Of course possibly society won't approve, but then they don't approve usually anyhow of much that is done, and it still goes on.

I had a line from Dr. DuBois in Los Angeles where he has been putting on a pageant. He will be back here around the 3rd of July. I am enclosing a program of the N.A.A.C.P. Program.

OPPORTUNITY
JOURNAL OF NEGRO LIFE
PUBLISHED BY THE NATIONAL URBAN LEAGUE
127 EAST 23RD STREET, NEW YORK CITY

OFFICE OF
CHARLES S. JOHNSON
EDITOR

    These are just off the press, so you ought to be the first one to have a copy in the Middle West. Mr. Walter White gave it to me. I had lunch with him on Wednesday and he autographed my copy of "The Fire in the Flint".

    Glad Mother liked the material. If she would like to, she can do whatever she wishes. Perhaps she would like to send it to one of her sisters in Sweden -- I've thought about them quite a bit recently. Are they all well? How about the one who has the little girl? I hope someday I can visit the land of the Midnight Sun with her and see all the places she has told us about so often.

                    Best regards,

                          Ethel

The Fire in the Flint
	by Walter White
There is Confusion
	by Jessie R. Fauset
The Gift of Black Folk
	by W. E. B. DuBois

The Penitent
	by Edna Worthley Underwood
The Passion-flower
	by Edna Worthley Underwood

Zora Neale Hurston: Preserving the Soul of Black Folklore

Zora Neale Hurston was one of the most vibrant and influential voices of the Harlem Renaissance, and she was celebrated for her ability to preserve and elevate Black Southern folklore through her storytelling and anthropological work. Her novels, such as *Their Eyes Were Watching God*, and her folklore collections are enduring testaments to the richness of Black cultural heritage. Hurston's magnetic personality and unapologetic embrace of her identity made her a beloved and electrifying presence in Harlem's artistic circles. Her relationship with Ethel Ray Nance exemplified the supportive and collaborative spirit that defined the Renaissance.

Dream Haven, the apartment Ethel shared with Regina Anderson Andrews and Louella Tucker, became a nurturing space for Hurston and other luminaries of the Harlem Renaissance. At these gatherings, Hurston's wit and charm captivated her audience, making her a beloved figure among her peers. Charles S. Johnson, the editor of *Opportunity: A Journal of Negro Life*, played a crucial role in supporting Hurston's career, introducing her to influential benefactors, including the prominent writer Fannie Hurst.

Ethel, closely connected to both Hurston and Johnson, recounted many anecdotes that highlighted Hurston's humor and resourcefulness. One particularly memorable incident occurred when Hurston was traveling with Fannie Hurst through the segregated South. As they approached a hotel that allowed only white patrons, Hurston knew they faced a dilemma. To ensure she could stay with Hurst, Hurston devised a clever plan: she disguised herself as an African woman who spoke no English.

A Seat at the Table: Ethel Ray Nance & the Harlem Renaissance

With her head wrapped in colorful cloth and her attire reflecting traditional African dress, Hurston approached the hotel desk with an air of confidence. When questioned by the staff, she communicated through gestures and a few borrowed phrases, effectively evading suspicion. This clever ruse not only showcased her quick thinking but also provided a poignant commentary on the absurdity of segregation. By navigating the complexities of racial discrimination with humor and ingenuity, Hurston exemplified her fearless spirit.

The experience not only highlighted Hurston's resourcefulness but also strengthened her bond with Hurst, who was deeply impressed by her ability to defy the oppressive social structures of the time. Such stories from Ethel exemplified how Hurston's adventures enriched her literary voice, allowing her to weave humor and social commentary into her work.

Through her experiences at Dream Haven and her interactions with figures like Johnson and Hurst, Hurston flourished as a writer, ultimately leading to the creation of her most famous work, *Their Eyes Were Watching God*. Her ability to blend humor with poignant social commentary made her a unique voice in American literature, and her legacy continues to inspire generations of writers and artists.

Ethel's relationship with Hurston was both dynamic and challenging, reflecting the complexities of managing a brilliant and unconventional personality. At the request of Charles S. Johnson, Ethel was tasked with ensuring that Hurston stayed focused on her commitments, particularly her work for *Opportunity*. Ethel took on this role with a sense of duty and admiration, recognizing Hurston's unique talent and the importance of her contributions to Black literature and culture. However, as Ethel recalled, Zora was "*hard to keep in bounds*." Hurston's boundless energy and penchant for improvisation made it a constant battle to keep her on schedule, but Ethel's steadfastness provided the structure Hurston often needed.

In a letter to her parents dated June 29, 1925, Ethel updates them on the events in Harlem, and pages 5 and 6 defend the role of literature in portraying life truthfully, even when it is uncomfortable. Though the letter is written to both her parents, the banter is most often between Ethel and her father, William. In this letter, she challenges his reluctance to embrace such portrayals and calls out the hypocrisy in how people judge morality and justice. Ethel also implicitly endorses Hurston's bold and uncompromising style, arguing that the power of storytelling lies in its ability to confront rather than shy away from the truth.

Hurston faced criticism for her bold and uncompromising style, primarily because her approach to storytelling and her themes often challenged prevailing social norms and expectations, particularly regarding race and gender. Her use of African American vernacular and folklore was groundbreaking, but it drew criticism from some contemporaries who believed her portrayal of Black life was overly simplistic or stereotypical. Critics like Richard Wright felt that her focus on cultural heritage and rural Southern life did not adequately address the harsh realities of urban Black experiences. Moreover, her willingness to confront hypocrisy—both within the Black community and in broader American society—was often seen as too provocative. She did not shy away from addressing issues such as class division, gender roles, and the complexities of Black identity, leading some to view her work as controversial or divisive.

A Seat at the Table: Ethel Ray Nance & the Harlem Renaissance

As a female writer in a predominantly male literary landscape, Hurston faced additional scrutiny. Her independent and assertive portrayal of women, particularly in works like *Their Eyes Were Watching God*, challenged traditional gender roles, which could alienate some audiences who were not ready to embrace such progressive views. Moreover, her unique narrative style—often interweaving dialect, humor, and rich cultural references—was sometimes dismissed as lacking the seriousness or gravitas expected in literature addressing racial issues, leading some critics to misunderstand the depth and significance of her work.

Despite these criticisms, Hurston's boldness in storytelling and her ability to confront hypocrisy ultimately contributed to her legacy as a pivotal figure in American literature. Her work has since been celebrated for its complexity, depth, and profound insights into the African American experience, demonstrating the enduring power of her voice. Ethel, in turn, played a crucial role in supporting Hurston's creative journey, offering her both practical guidance and a nurturing environment to develop her ideas. Together, they exemplified the power of friendship, collaboration, and cultural preservation in shaping one of the most influential movements in American history.

Ethel's relationships with Zora Neale Hurston and Fauset Redmon Fauset reflected the diversity of thought and expression within the Renaissance. Hurston's folkloric storytelling and Fauset's polished prose offered contrasting yet complementary perspectives on Black life. Ethel worked alongside Fauset at *Opportunity* and *The Crisis*, supporting her editorial efforts to elevate Black women writers.

Through their partnership, Ethel and Hurston celebrated the richness of Black cultural heritage and inspired generations to embrace and honor their roots. Zora Neale Hurston's legacy as a keeper of folklore and a master storyteller continues to resonate, ensuring her place as one of the most enduring figures of the Renaissance and a beloved figure in Ethel Ray Nance's circle of influence.

Literary Crossroads: Zora Neale Hurston and Fauset Redmon Fauset

Ethel's relationships with Zora Neale Hurston and Fauset Redmon Fauset reflected the diversity of thought and expression within the Renaissance. Hurston's folkloric storytelling and Fauset's polished prose offered contrasting yet complementary perspectives on Black life. Ethel worked alongside Fauset at *Opportunity* and the *Crisis*, supporting her editorial efforts to elevate Black women writers. Hurston, with her infectious energy and dedication to preserving Black cultural heritage, found a kindred spirit in Ethel. Together, they represented the dynamic range of voices that made the Renaissance a transformative cultural movement.

This same spirit of artistic collaboration and cultural pride was reflected in Ethel's connection with Gwendolyn Bennett, a multifaceted artist, poet, and educator whose contributions to the Harlem Renaissance were marked by her celebration of Black identity, culture, and resilience. Bennett's work, which spanned poetry, visual art, and essays, provided a deeply evocative exploration of themes like love, nature, and social justice.

A Seat at the Table: Ethel Ray Nance & the Harlem Renaissance

Gwendolyn Bennett: A Creative Force Across Mediums

Brooks's creative output appeared in prominent publications such as *Opportunity* and *The Crisis*, where she became a vital voice advocating for the beauty and complexity of African American life. Like her relationships with Hurston and Fauset, Ethel's friendship with Bennett underscored the interconnectedness of the Harlem Renaissance, where individuals worked together to elevate Black voices and foster cultural pride.

Bennett's poetry often drew from the rhythms of nature and the emotional depth of human experience, blending personal reflection with broader cultural themes. Her well-known works, such as "To a Dark Girl" and "Heritage," celebrated the beauty and strength of Black women and the enduring connection to African roots. In these poems, Bennett's use of vivid imagery and lyrical language creates a sense of intimacy and reverence for the past. Ethel, who admired Bennett's ability to articulate the complexities of identity through poetry, found inspiration in her friend's work. For Ethel, Bennett's art was a testament to the transformative power of creativity in challenging stereotypes and promoting pride in one's heritage.

In addition to her writing, Bennett was an accomplished visual artist whose work reflected her love of African and African American traditions. Her illustrations and designs often graced the covers of Renaissance publications, adding a visual dimension to the literary movement. Bennett's dual talent as a writer and artist embodied the Renaissance's ethos of multidisciplinary expression, where creativity knew no bounds. Ethel, who worked closely with artists and writers through her roles at *Opportunity* and other organizations, admired Bennett's ability to excel across various forms of expression, seeing her as a model of artistic versatility.

Bennett's influence extended beyond her creative works. She played an active role in organizing events that brought together the intellectual and artistic elite of Harlem. Her leadership in planning gatherings, lectures, and exhibitions helped create spaces for Black artists to share their work and ideas. These events fostered a sense of community and collaboration that was central to the Renaissance's success. Ethel and Bennett likely crossed paths at these gatherings, where they connected over their shared commitment to supporting and amplifying Black voices. Ethel appreciated Bennett's dedication to mentoring younger artists, recognizing her as a figure who not only created but also nurtured creativity in others.

One of Bennett's most significant contributions was her role as an educator. She taught at Howard University and other institutions, where she inspired a new generation of artists and thinkers. Her work as a teacher reflected her belief in the power of education to uplift and empower the Black community. Ethel, who valued education and mentorship as key components of cultural preservation, found common ground with Bennett in their mutual desire to foster talent and inspire change.

Ethel's connection to Bennett highlighted the interconnectedness of the Renaissance's key figures. While Ethel worked to document and facilitate the work of artists and writers, Bennett embodied the movement's creative and intellectual energy. Their friendship exemplified the spirit of collaboration that defined the Harlem Renaissance, where individuals supported and inspired one another to reach greater heights.

Bennett's poetry often struck a personal chord with Ethel, who admired her ability to capture the emotional depth of the Black experience. Ethel recalled moments when Bennett's words resonated deeply during gatherings at Dream Haven. Bennett's presence at these gatherings brought a sense of warmth and wisdom as she shared her insights into art, culture, and the human condition. Ethel cherished these interactions, which deepened her appreciation for Bennett's work and reinforced her belief in the power of art to foster connection and understanding.

One of Bennett's most notable qualities was her ability to bridge different artistic disciplines and cultural influences. She often incorporated African motifs and themes into her work, blending traditional elements with modernist aesthetics. This approach mirrored the Renaissance's larger effort to reclaim African heritage and integrate it into contemporary expressions of Black identity. Ethel admired Bennett's ability to honor the past while embracing the possibilities of the present, seeing her as a beacon of cultural pride and innovation.

Bennett's essays and editorials in publications like *Opportunity* reflected her commitment to social justice and equality. She wrote passionately about the challenges faced by African Americans, using her platform to advocate for change. Her eloquence and conviction made her a respected voice within the Renaissance, and her work often sparked important conversations about race, identity, and representation. Ethel, who was deeply involved in the operations of *Opportunity*, recognized the importance of Bennett's contributions and supported her efforts to elevate these critical issues.

Despite the challenges of being a Black female artist in a predominantly white, male-dominated society, Bennett's resilience and creativity shone brightly. She navigated these obstacles with grace and determination, earning the admiration of her peers, including Ethel. Their friendship was a testament to the strength of the bonds forged during the Harlem Renaissance, where shared goals and mutual respect created a foundation for lasting connections.

Ethel often reflected on the impact of Bennett's work and their shared experiences during this transformative period. She saw Bennett as a trailblazer who used her talents to celebrate Black identity and challenge societal norms. Bennett's ability to inspire and uplift others left an indelible mark on Ethel, who carried these lessons into her own work as a writer, activist, and advocate for cultural preservation.

Through her poetry, visual art, essays, and mentorship, Gwendolyn Bennett left an enduring legacy as one of the Harlem Renaissance's most versatile and influential figures. Her relationship with Ethel Ray Nance underscored the importance of collaboration and community in driving the movement's success. Together, they exemplified the Renaissance's commitment to celebrating Black culture and empowering future generations through art, education, and activism.

A Seat at the Table: Ethel Ray Nance & the Harlem Renaissance

For Ethel, Bennett represented the spirit of the Harlem Renaissance, a celebration of creativity, resilience, and the beauty of Black identity. Their friendship and shared dedication to cultural preservation remain a testament to the transformative power of art and the enduring impact of collaboration in shaping history.

Karen Felecia Nance

Eric Walrond: Bringing the Caribbean and Harlem

Photo of Eric Walrond, (undated) collection of Karen Felecia Nance

Eric Walrond was a vital literary voice of the Harlem Renaissance, whose sharp journalistic style and evocative storytelling captured the complexities of the Black diaspora. His writing, which spanned short stories, novels, and journalism, illuminated the struggles and triumphs of Caribbean and African

American communities, forging a link between Harlem and the broader Atlantic world. His relationship with Ethel was one of mutual respect and collaboration, rooted in their shared belief in the global significance of the Harlem Renaissance. Their professional and intellectual partnership spanned years, beginning in Kansas City and continuing in Harlem, where they both worked to uplift Black artists, writers, and thinkers.

Ethel first met Walrond in October 1923 while working as the office manager for the Urban League during its Annual Meeting in Kansas City. The event brought together key figures in Black activism, literature, and social work, and it was here that she was introduced to Walrond, whose energy and intellect left a lasting impression. At the time, Walrond was already making a name for himself as a writer and journalist, contributing to major Black publications such as *The Crisis* and *Opportunity*. Their initial meeting in Kansas City marked the beginning of a professional relationship that would deepen once Ethel moved to New York.

On May 14, 1924, when Ethel arrived in New York City, she was greeted at Grand Central Station by Charles S. Johnson, Madeline Allison, and Walrond. By this point, Walrond had become the business manager of *Opportunity*, where he played a crucial role in shaping the magazine's success. His work in this capacity extended beyond business operations; he was a key editor and contributor whose insights into race, colonialism, and diasporic identity helped define the publication's tone. Having maintained their connection since Kansas City, Walrond was instrumental in helping Ethel navigate Harlem's cultural and literary scene.

Ethel and Walrond often attended gatherings at *Dream Haven*, where their discussions reinforced their shared belief that the Harlem Renaissance was not solely an American movement but a global one. Walrond's writings, particularly his short story collection *Tropic Death*, reflected this diasporic consciousness. His stories, filled with themes of displacement, colonialism, and resilience, resonated deeply with Ethel, who saw his work as a testament to the transatlantic ties that bound Black communities together. Ethel provided Walrond with constructive feedback, helping him refine his narratives and strengthen his impact as a writer. She admired his ability to confront harsh realities with poetic eloquence, further cementing his legacy as a critical voice of the Renaissance.

Walrond had an uncanny ability to recognize the importance of a story in real-time. His journalistic instincts were sharp; he "*knew a headline when he saw one in the making, a half a note away,*" as one contemporary described him. He never spoiled a good story, and he had a knack for making friends easily. In Harlem, he was known for being the person to contact when one wanted to meet interesting people. If someone wished to enter Harlem's literary and artistic circles, they were often advised to "*get in touch with Walrond,*" who would ensure they were introduced to the right people.

Ethel, who had a similar role as a connector in Harlem's literary world, found in Walrond a kindred spirit. They both understood that the Renaissance was as much about relationships and networks as it was about individual artistic achievement. They regularly attended gatherings hosted by Charles S. Johnson, where they, along with figures like Aaron Douglas, strategized ways to harness the cultural momentum surrounding them. These were not just casual social events but planning sessions that laid the groundwork for something much larger.

One of the most significant events that emerged from these discussions was the *Opportunity* Dinner at the Civic Club on March 21, 1924. Ethel played a crucial role in organizing the dinner, ensuring that it proceeded seamlessly, while Walrond, in his role at *Opportunity*, helped set the intellectual tone for the evening. The event forged connections between artists, writers, and benefactors, solidifying *Opportunity* as the leading platform for Black intellectual and artistic expression.

Beyond his contributions to *Opportunity*, Walrond moved into broader publishing circles. He often spent time downtown at *Esquire Magazine*, *Theatre Arts*, and *Munsey Magazine*, always eager to share his experiences upon returning to Harlem. Ethel and others in their circle often joked that Walrond seemed to seek out encounters with discrimination, knowing that every incident would result in a compelling article. His sharp observations on race and society made him one of the most incisive journalists of the era.

Despite his literary success, Walrond's later career was marked by struggle. He received prestigious recognition, including the Harmon Foundation Award for achievement in literature and the Zona Gale Scholarship to study creative writing at the University of Wisconsin. However, these opportunities did not yield the long-term success he had hoped for. He was unable to fully capitalize on the scholarship, as well as a Guggenheim fellowship, and ultimately did not return to America after leaving for England in 1931. His departure marked the end of an era in Harlem, though his legacy endured through the writers and thinkers he had influenced.

Ethel, who remained close to Walrond throughout his time in Harlem, reflected on his impact with deep appreciation. She recognized his role in holding their literary circle together, as he had an unmatched ability to bring people together and introduce new talent to the community. His independence, his journalistic timing, and his relentless energy made him an unforgettable presence in Harlem's intellectual circles. Though he eventually distanced himself from the movement, his work continued to shape discussions on race, identity, and the global dimensions of Black literature.

One of the most interesting aspects of Walrond's personality was his skepticism toward certain figures in the Renaissance, particularly Carl Van Vechten. Unlike many in Harlem who welcomed Van Vechten's fascination with Black culture, Walrond saw him as an outsider who merely observed rather than truly engaged with the community. His only close associate from that group was Charles S. Johnson, whom he deeply respected. Walrond instead built strong relationships with other influential West Indian intellectuals like Arturo Schomburg and Cooper Holstein, both of whom played important roles in supporting Black writers.

Ethel's friendship with Walrond was one of mutual admiration and intellectual exchange. She believed in his literary voice, just as she had believed in Aaron Douglas's artistic talent. Her feedback and encouragement helped refine his work, while his sharp insights into diasporic identity expanded her own understanding of the

Renaissance's global scope. Their relationship exemplified the importance of collaboration and mentorship in Harlem's creative movement.

Eric Walrond's legacy as a journalist, novelist, and literary figure remains one of the most compelling aspects of the Harlem Renaissance. His ability to navigate both the artistic and journalistic worlds, his deep engagement with diasporic themes, and his charismatic personality made him a cornerstone of the movement. Ethel Ray Nance's connection to him highlights her own role as a bridge between intellectuals, ensuring that their voices were heard and their stories preserved.

Through her friendship with Walrond, Ethel saw firsthand the power of literature to shape cultural identity and challenge societal norms. His *Tropic Death* was a reflection of the struggles and triumphs of Black communities across the world, reinforcing her belief that the Renaissance was an international movement. Walrond's departure from America marked the end of their shared Harlem years, but the impact of their collaboration endured, leaving a lasting imprint on the legacy of Black literature.

Claude Barnett and Aaron Douglas: They called her "Jimmie" ~ The Visionary & the Artist.

Photo: Individuals have names written: Jimmie, John C Ed. 1923, Kansas City, Missouri; Private collection of Karen Felecia Nance

One of the unsolved mysteries of Ethel Ray Nance's past is the origin of the name "Jimmie." This is the only known photograph that identifies her as such, taken in 1923 at the Kansas City Urban League's Annual Conference. The man in the middle, identified as "John," bears a strong resemblance to the man in the Kansas City Urban League's 1924 photo in Chapter 6, and the woman on the right, "Ed," closely resembles the woman standing at the far right in the breakfast party photo from the YMCA gathering on October 18-23, 1924, in Kansas City, Missouri.

A Seat at the Table: Ethel Ray Nance & the Harlem Renaissance

During their lifetimes, both Claude Barnett and Aaron Douglas referred to Ethel as "Jimmie," reinforcing the likelihood that they not only met her in Kansas City but also developed a familiarity and respect for her that endured beyond their initial introduction. The consistent use of this name suggests an intimate professional or personal relationship, one that may have been cultivated through shared intellectual and cultural endeavors. Given Barnett's role in Black journalism and Douglas's influence in visual arts, their engagement with Ethel may have extended beyond mere acquaintance—possibly collaborating on initiatives or discussions that shaped their respective contributions to the Harlem Renaissance and African American advocacy.

Barnett, Douglas, and Ethel were in Kansas City in 1923 for significant reasons tied to their respective careers and interests. Claude Barnett, as the founder of the Associated Negro Press (ANP), was also likely there to cover or engage with the Urban League's efforts to improve social and economic conditions for African Americans. His work required constant travel to major cities where Black intellectuals, journalists, and activists gathered.

Meanwhile, Aaron Douglas had recently begun his teaching career at Lincoln High School in Kansas City, a premier institution for Black students at a time when segregation limited educational opportunities. His position placed him at the center of a growing cultural and intellectual movement. Ethel Ray Nance, an emerging activist and writer, was deeply involved with the Urban League and other organizations seeking to uplift Black communities through education and economic empowerment. The Kansas City Urban League's Annual Conference in 1923 was a major event, bringing together leading figures in civil rights, journalism, and education—making it an ideal setting for Barnett, Douglas, and Ethel to interact and form lasting professional connections.

Barnett and Douglas's shared nickname for Ethel, "Jimmie," likely reflected their appreciation for her tenacity, practicality, and ability to navigate diverse social circles. Whether the name stemmed from an inside joke, a term of endearment, or a recognition of her behind-the-scenes influence, it underscored the deep respect they held for her.

By 1924, Ethel had moved to New York to join Charles S. Johnson's staff at *Opportunity* magazine, further embedding herself in the Harlem Renaissance's literary and cultural circles. As a researcher, she reviewed manuscripts, edited news items, and coordinated special projects, including a Harlem-focused issue of *Survey Graphic*. It was in this role that she advocated Aaron Douglas's talent, recognizing his artistic potential and persuading him to come to Harlem. Douglas, initially hesitant to leave Kansas City, aspired to study art in Paris instead. However, Ethel persistently encouraged him, famously writing, "It's better to wash dishes in New York than be president of a high school in Kansas City." Eventually, Douglas relented, arriving in Harlem and staying temporarily at 580 St. Nicholas Street, the apartment Ethel shared with Regina Anderson and Louella Tucker at Dream Haven.

Through Ethel's influence, Douglas connected with influential figures like W.E.B. Du Bois, who secured him a job in the shipping department at *The Crisis*, providing him with a foothold in Harlem's artistic community. Ethel also introduced Douglas's work to Winold

Reiss, a German artist collaborating with Johnson on *Survey Graphic*. Reiss was impressed with Douglas's sketches and recommended him for broader opportunities, leading to Douglas's contributions to *The New Negro* and establishing his legacy as the "Father of Black American Art."

Ethel's relentless advocacy for Douglas transformed his career. Her belief in his potential gave him the courage to pursue artistic ambitions in Harlem, a decision that led to the creation of some of his most celebrated works. Douglas's murals at the Schomburg Center for Research in Black Culture and Fisk University embodied the Renaissance's spirit of cultural pride and progress. His distinct visual language, blending African motifs with modernist techniques, captured the essence of Black resilience and achievement, serving as a visual counterpart to the Renaissance's literary works.

Beyond her role in Douglas's career, Ethel played an essential part in Harlem's artistic and intellectual community. As Johnson's talent scout, she identified promising writers and artists, ensuring that new voices were given opportunities to thrive. She often offered her home as a temporary refuge for emerging talents like Douglas and Zora Neale Hurston, fostering a collaborative environment where creativity flourished.

Douglas's and Barnett's shared commitment to amplifying Black voices—through art and journalism, respectively—made their contributions complementary. Barnett's *Associated Negro Press* provided coverage of the Harlem Renaissance, ensuring that the movement reached a broad audience, while Douglas's art visually defined the era's aesthetics. Ethel, acting as a bridge between these influential figures, played a crucial role in fostering their collaborations and expanding the Renaissance's impact.

The relationship between Barnett and Douglas represents the interconnectedness of the Harlem Renaissance. Their shared mission to elevate Black culture created a synergy that enriched the movement's cultural output. Barnett's role in amplifying the written word and Douglas's ability to give visual form to the Renaissance's ideals were complementary contributions to a larger narrative of empowerment and resilience.

In many ways, Ethel Ray Nance was the glue that connected these influential figures. Her foresight, determination, and unwavering belief in Black artistic and journalistic talent helped shape the Harlem Renaissance. The nickname "Jimmie," bestowed upon her by both Barnett and Douglas, stands as a testament to her indispensable role in the era's cultural awakening. Through her efforts, Barnett and Douglas were able to make enduring contributions to the Harlem Renaissance, leaving legacies that continue to inspire future generations.

A Seat at the Table: Ethel Ray Nance & the Harlem Renaissance

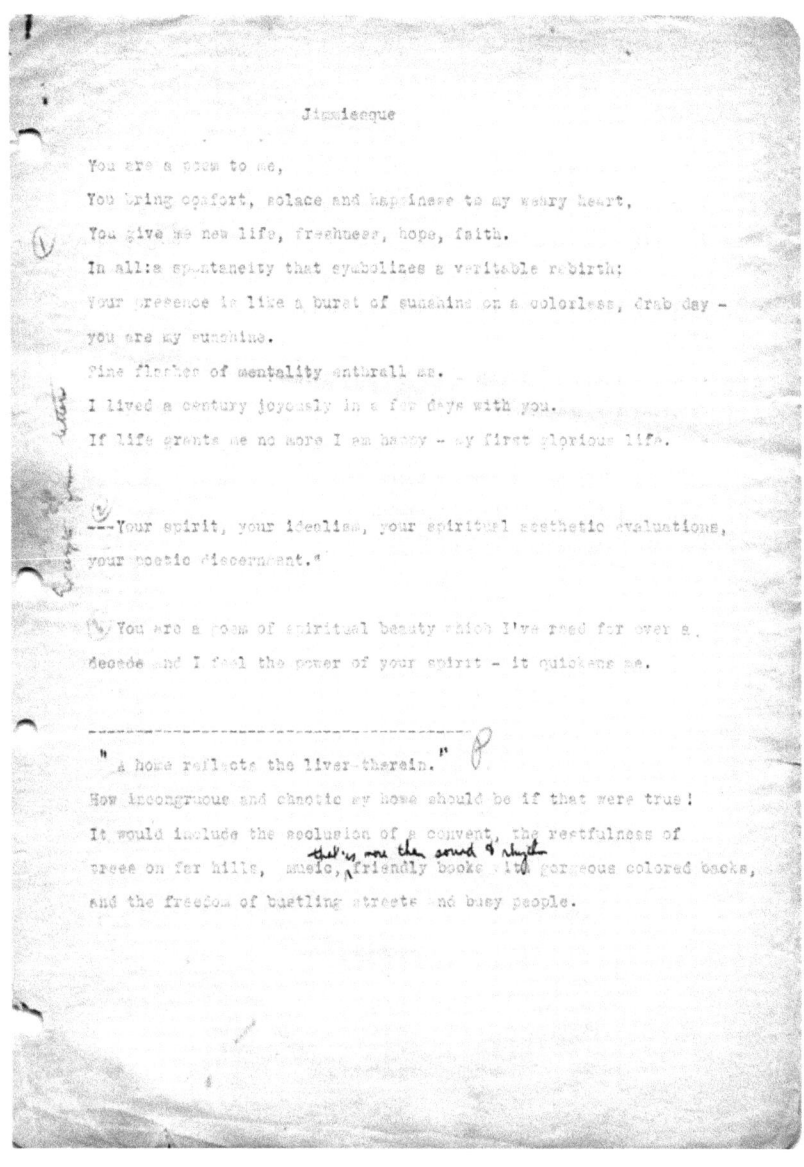

Jimmiesque

You are a poem to me,
You bring comfort, solace and happiness to my weary heart,
You give me new life, freshness, hope, faith.
In all: a spontaneity that symbolizes a veritable rebirth;
Your presence is like a burst of sunshine on a colorless, drab day —
you are my sunshine.
Fine flashes of mentality enthrall me.
I lived a century joyously in a few days with you.
If life grants me no more I am happy — my first glorious life.

"—Your spirit, your idealism, your spiritual aesthetic evaluations, your poetic discernment."

"You are a poem of spiritual beauty which I've read for over a decade and I feel the power of your spirit — it quickens me."

"A home reflects the liver-therein."
How incongruous and chaotic my home should be if that were true!
It would include the seclusion of a convent, the restfulness of trees on far hills, music, *that is, not the sound of rhythm* friendly books with gorgeous colored backs, and the freedom of bustling streets and busy people.

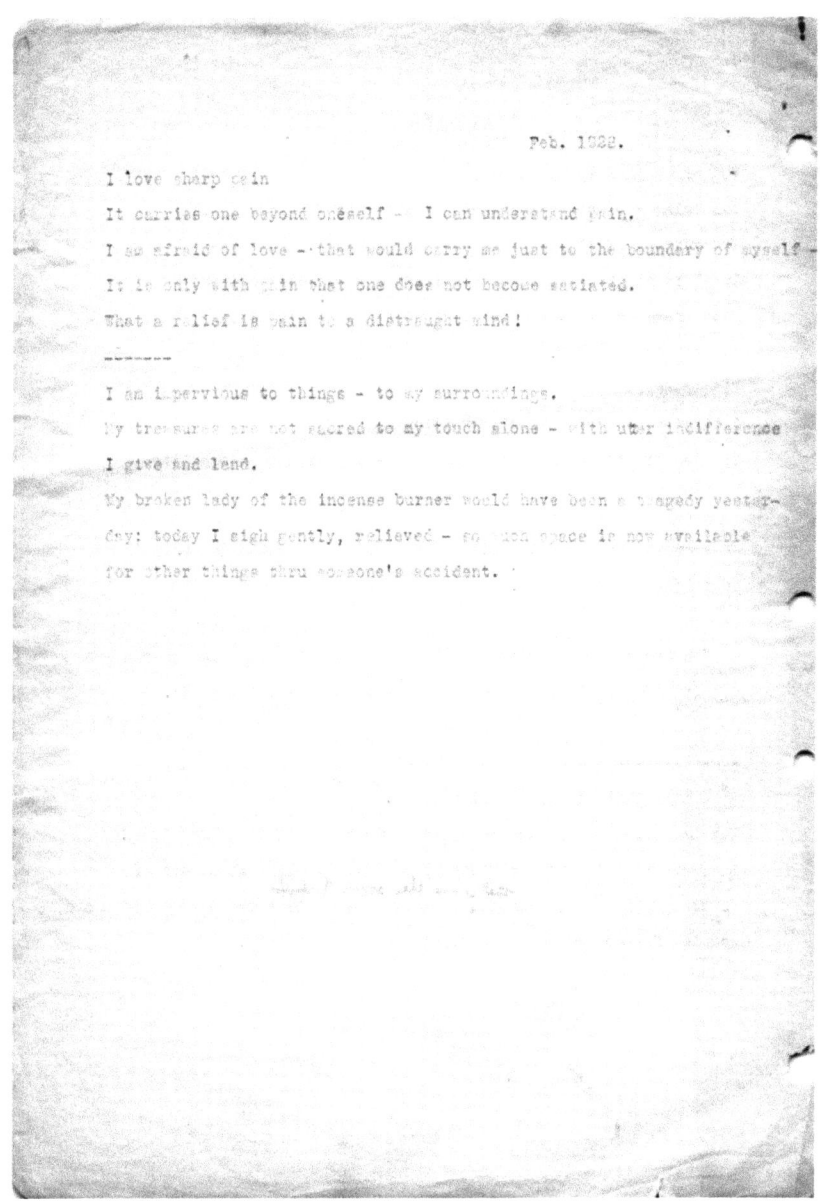

Poem entitled "Jimmiesque" author not identified, and other notes: Private collection of Karen Felecia Nance

A Seat at the Table: Ethel Ray Nance & the Harlem Renaissance

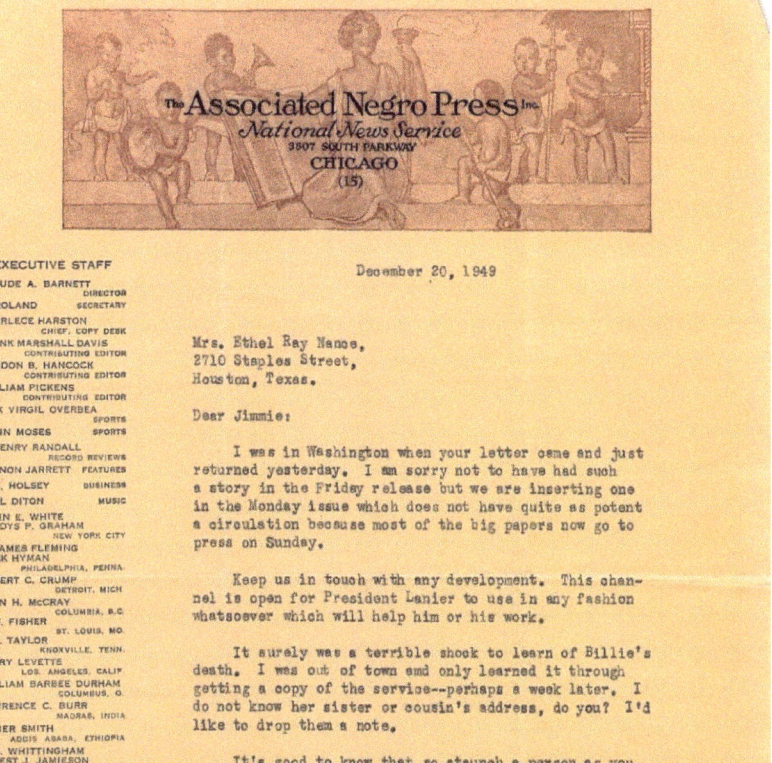

Letter from Claude A. Barnett to "Jimmie" dated December 20, 1949, Private collection of Karen Felecia Nance

Karen Felecia Nance

FISK UNIVERSITY
NASHVILLE 8, TENNESSEE

DEPARTMENT OF ART

May 18, 1969

Dear Jimmie:

How terrible to have been so near you without seeing you. I forgot all about it: Maxwells being in the vicinity. I could easily have arranged to spend a day with them.

I was the house guest of the Cowles, who commissioned me to paint the portrait of Mrs. Bethune. They are both quite wonderful people. The trip was a big moment for me and it would have been appropriate for you to have shared it with me.

Would love to see you before you go back to the coast. I'll do my best.

I am enclosing a small clipping you might like to see.

All the best to the Maxwells.

Sincerely,
Doug

Letter from Aaron Douglas to "Jimmie" dated May 18, 1969, Private collection of Karen Felecia Nance

A Seat at the Table: Ethel Ray Nance & the Harlem Renaissance

Shared Legacies: The Philosopher, the Labor Leader & Activist, and the Historian & Poet
Alain Locke: The Philosopher of the Renaissance

Alain Locke, often called the "Father of the Harlem Renaissance," was a philosopher, literary critic, and editor whose anthology *The New Negro* (1925) provided a manifesto for the movement. His work emphasized the importance of art as a means of cultural and social transformation, encouraging Black artists and writers to draw inspiration from their African heritage while asserting their modern identity. By articulating the ideals of the Harlem Renaissance, Locke helped shape the philosophical framework that guided its artists and intellectuals.

Ethel's relationship with Locke was instrumental in supporting the publication of *The New Negro*, a fact later recognized in a 1933 article in *The Chicago Defender*. The article described Ethel, then known as Mrs. Ethel Ray Williams, as *"one of the most popular of the artistic-intelligentsia group which was at its height in New York about the time of the publication of The New Negro, edited by Dr. Locke, and in the making of which Mrs. Williams had, if not a hand, at least a finger."* This acknowledgment affirms her role in assisting Locke in assembling and promoting what would become one of the most influential literary collections of the Harlem Renaissance.

Ethel's work with *Opportunity* magazine positioned her at the center of Harlem's literary network, giving her direct access to many of the writers and thinkers featured in *The New Negro*. As a trusted associate of Charles S. Johnson, she was actively involved in curating, organizing, and promoting Black literary voices. It is likely that her editorial work, administrative support, and relationships with key figures such as Langston Hughes, Countee Cullen, and Aaron Douglas facilitated Locke's ability to bring *The New Negro* to life.

Beyond her contributions to the anthology, Ethel admired Locke's ability to inspire collective action among creatives. His emphasis on using art to elevate and redefine Black identity resonated deeply with her, reinforcing her belief in the power of literature and visual art to reshape societal perceptions. Locke's influence extended beyond his writing; he was a mentor to many young artists and thinkers, and his guidance helped shape the careers of figures like Douglas and Hughes, both of whom Ethel also supported.

A. Philip Randolph: The Labor Leader and Activist

A. Philip Randolph was a pioneering labor leader and civil rights activist whose work extended the Renaissance's goals of equity into the realm of labor and social justice. As the founder of the Brotherhood of Sleeping Car Porters, the first Black-led labor union, Randolph fought for the rights of African American workers and challenged systemic economic inequalities. His activism extended into civil rights, where he played a key role in pressuring President Roosevelt to issue Executive Order 8802, which banned racial discrimination in the defense industry during World War II.

A Seat at the Table: Ethel Ray Nance & the Harlem Renaissance

Ethel's relationship with Randolph was rooted in their shared commitment to justice and empowerment. Through her work with *Opportunity* and the Urban League, Ethel often engaged with leading activists who sought systemic change. She admired Randolph's ability to merge economic advocacy with racial justice, recognizing that progress in one area could not be achieved without the other. Though their interactions were primarily through Harlem's intellectual and activist circles, Ethel saw in Randolph a model of determination, using strategic organization and advocacy to create lasting change.

Ethel first met Randolph during her trip with her father in 1919. They visited the *Messenger* office when they were in New York and met Randolph, then served as the publication president. Ethel recorded her impressions of Randolph in her journal, noting that he was "a very able speaker, clear, concise, unwavering in his views, which are considered radical by readers." Despite these perceptions, Ethel herself "couldn't detect much radicalism" in his views.

This early encounter foreshadowed the alignment of their efforts in later years, as both worked within Harlem's intellectual and activist circles to advance racial and economic justice. Randolph, like Locke, believed in the power of collective action. While Locke encouraged Black artists to define their own cultural identity, Randolph fought for economic independence and fair labor rights. Both men sought to uplift Black communities by empowering individuals within their respective fields—art and labor. Their visions intersected in the belief that African Americans must take control of their own narratives and opportunities, whether through artistic expression or organized labor.

Karen Felecia Nance

Arna Bontemps: Chronicling History Through Poetry

Arna Bontemps chronicled Black history through poetry and literature. His works, such as *God Sends Sunday* and *The Story of the Negro,* provided a rich historical context for the Renaissance. Bontemps's collaborations with Langston Hughes, including their play *Mulatto,* underscored the era's interconnected creative energy.

Bontemps met Ethel when he attended a gathering at Dream Haven, where they exchanged ideas and fostered a shared appreciation for literature. It was also at Dream Haven that Bontemps met Langston Hughes, a meeting that would spark one of the Harlem Renaissance's most significant literary collaborations. Hughes was celebrated for his jazz-infused poetry and profound connection to the Black experience, and he found a kindred spirit in Bontemps. Their friendship led to a lifetime of creative exchanges that enriched the cultural and literary fabric of the movement.

Bontemps's dedication to preserving Black history resonated with Ethel's advocacy for cultural preservation, creating a lasting bond. His meticulous approach to documenting the Black experience complemented Alain Locke's philosophical framing of the Renaissance and A. Philip Randolph's fight for economic justice. Each, in their own way, worked toward empowering Black communities through knowledge, culture, and advocacy.

Bontemps later referenced Ethel in his book *Harlem Renaissance Remembered*, further underscoring her vital role in fostering connections and creativity during this transformative era. His work, like that of his contemporaries, continues to shape historical discourse and inspire new generations of scholars and writers dedicated to Black cultural heritage.

Shared Legacies: Locke, Randolph, and Bontemps

While Alain Locke, A. Philip Randolph, and Arna Bontemps operated in different spheres, philosophy, labor, and literature, they shared a common goal: the elevation of Black identity and empowerment. Locke sought to define Black artistic and intellectual identity, Randolph fought for economic justice, and Bontemps preserved Black history through storytelling. Their combined efforts provided a foundation for the Harlem Renaissance and the broader Civil Rights Movement, ensuring that Black voices were not only heard but also respected and uplifted.

Ethel's role in these intersections highlights her unique ability to bring together intellectuals, activists, and artists. She was more than just a witness to history; she was an active participant, shaping the conversations that defined an era. The Harlem Renaissance thrived on collaboration, and through her friendships with Locke, Randolph, and Bontemps, Ethel played a crucial role in sustaining the movement's momentum, ensuring that its ideals of cultural pride, economic justice, and historical preservation endured beyond Harlem's golden age.

Countee Cullen: The Poet's Elegance

Countee Cullen was one of the most refined and lyrical voices of the Harlem Renaissance, blending classical poetic forms with themes of racial identity, love, and beauty. His poetry, which included works such as *Color* (1925) and *Heritage* (1925), reflected a deep yearning for racial unity and cultural appreciation. Unlike Langston Hughes, who embraced Black vernacular and jazz rhythms, Cullen's work leaned toward a more traditional literary style, drawing inspiration from European poets while addressing the realities of Black life.

Ethel developed a close friendship with Cullen, describing him as *"(a) quiet and kind (person) adding: (he) never hurt anyone."* Unlike some of the more flamboyant figures of the Renaissance, Cullen carried himself with an air of gentility, which Ethel deeply appreciated. He had been raised by loving foster parents, to whom he felt an immense sense of responsibility. This strong familial bond influenced his demeanor and the way he navigated social spaces, often with caution and reserve. His attachment to his foster parents made him more mindful of his actions, and he was particularly careful about his public image.

Ethel and her circle of friends, including Regina Andrews and others at *Dream Haven*, were surprised to learn that, despite having written about Harlem nightlife, Cullen had never actually been to a cabaret. Though his poetry painted vivid images of beautiful brown girls dancing in such settings, he had never personally experienced them. Ethel and her friends decided that this had to change. To celebrate his graduation from New York University, they hosted a dinner in his honor, which also served as an informal substitute for the school's official ceremony. Afterward, they took Cullen to his very first cabaret.

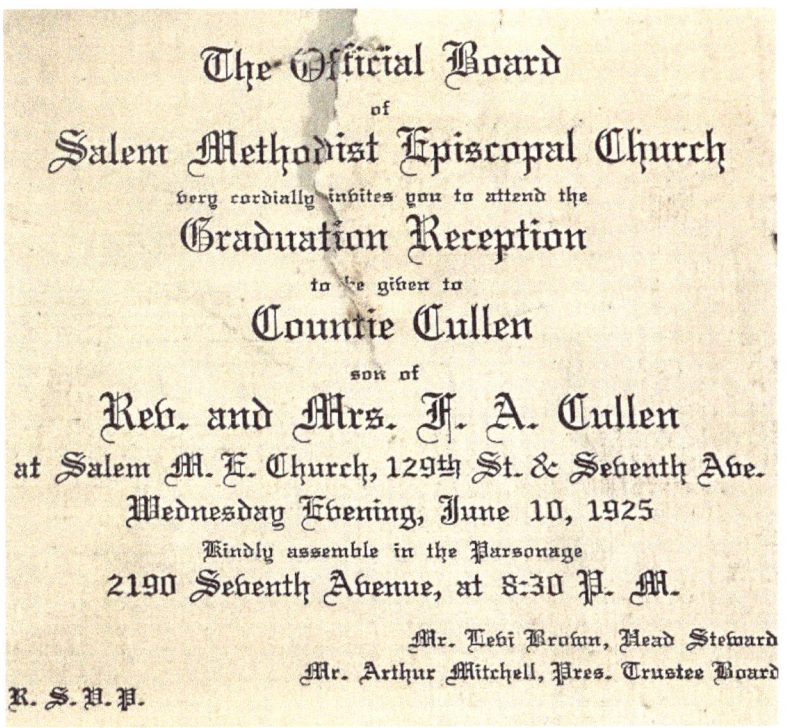

Countie Cullen's College Graduation Invitation 1925, Private collection of Karen Felecia Nance

Their destination was a cozy, tucked-away venue on Upper Fifth Avenue, down a flight of stairs, which they affectionately called *The Cat on the Saxophone.* It was likely one of Harlem's original small cabarets, known for its intimate performances and vibrant atmosphere. Cullen was enchanted by everything—the music, the dancing, and the rich energy of the room. He was particularly taken by a charming waitress named Melody, who, in addition to serving guests, would occasionally sing for them. The entire evening was an exhilarating introduction to the world he had so poetically imagined but never experienced firsthand.

Ethel's gesture of bringing Cullen into this space underscored her nurturing nature and her deep care for the people in her life. While Cullen was undoubtedly an intellectual giant, his sheltered upbringing had left gaps in his firsthand knowledge of the very world he so beautifully described in his poetry. Ethel and her friends saw this moment as a way to broaden his perspective, immersing him in the vibrancy of Harlem's nightlife while ensuring that he felt comfortable and welcomed.

Their friendship extended beyond this singular experience. Cullen frequently visited *Dream Haven*, where he found a warm and supportive environment for discussing his poetry. He valued Ethel's opinion, as she had an intuitive sense of literary merit and understood the importance of shaping narratives that reflected the richness of Black life. Ethel admired Cullen for more than just his literary prowess, and she respected his integrity, his quiet dignity, and his unwavering commitment to his craft. Though Harlem was filled with loud and larger-than-life personalities, Cullen's reserved nature set him apart. In him, Ethel saw a poet who, despite his careful approach to life, was unafraid to explore the complexities of Black identity through verse.

Ethel made the first cuts on submissions in *Opportunity's* literary contest in 1925, handled negotiations with the panel of judges, gave Charles S. Johnson many ideas for the awards dinner, and oversaw the seating arrangements at the Fifth Avenue

Restaurant. At the dinner, she and Regina shared a table with two of the winners: Countie Cullen and Langston Hughes, both frequent visitors to the Dream Haven.

Cullen's humility only added to this appeal as he navigated the dynamic world of Harlem's intellectuals and creatives. At Dream Haven, his poems sparked discussions about the intersection of art and social justice, themes that echoed throughout the Renaissance. Ethel and her companions were often astonished at how Cullen could distill intricate ideas into his elegant verses, offering their feedback and encouragement with every visit.

Ethel enrolled in a Short Story Course at Columbia University in 1924-25, at the same time Dr. Du Bois's daughter, Yolande, was enrolled in the Master of Arts program. Countie Countee earned his bachelor's degree from New York University. Even after Ethel left Harlem in 1925, she remained close. She was invited to his wedding with Yolande Du Bois on April 9, 1928. Ethel was delighted to receive the invitation, which included a handwritten note from Dr. Du Bois: "Admit within the ribbons of the church. "Though she was unable to attend, she noted in her journal that "from all accounts, it was an extraordinary event with 16 bridesmaids, etc." The wedding had 1,200 invited guests, with more than 3,000 in attendance.

Ethel's invitation to Nina & Countie's wedding in 1928, Private collection of Karen Felecia Nance

Cullen continued to correspond with Ethel over the years. In a letter dated September 4, 1934, from his home at 2190 Seventh Avenue in New York City, he wrote:

Dear Ethel, I do extend my greetings and good wishes to Glenn Ray (Ethel's son, born July 2, 1934), about whom I just learned on reaching home again a few days after six weeks in Europe. If his life is as royal as his announcement of his advent, it won't be the stale thing to most of his elders. All good wishes to you.

Sincerely,

Countee Cullen

A Seat at the Table: Ethel Ray Nance & the Harlem Renaissance

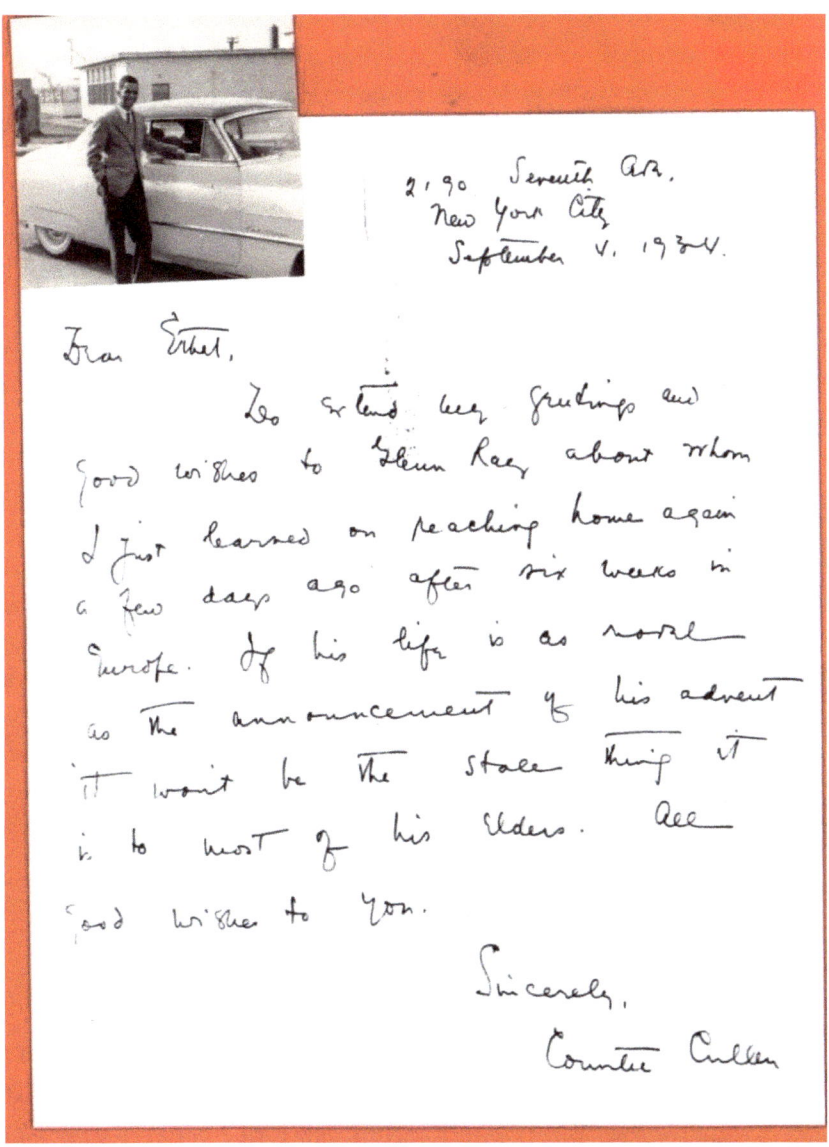

Letter to Ethel from Countie Cullen dated September 4. 1934, Private collection of Karen Felecia Nance

```
                --oOo--
Designer - Leroy A. H. Williams,

Production Manager - Ethel Ray Williams,

Technical Assistant - Dr. Pennie,           The 1934 Model

Model Released - July 2, 1934.              of the

Make - Boy.                                 Leroy A. H. Williams
                                                  Company.
Weight - 7 lbs. 15 oz.
                                                    ---
Wheelbase - 20½ inches.                     Duluth, Minnesota.

Name - Glenn Ray Williams.

Upholstery - White Outing Flannel
             in Gahndi style.
Lights - Blue.
                                            _____
                                            The Management assures the public
                                            that there will be no more new
Free squeeling,  Two lung power,            models released during the balance
Economical feed, Changable seat covers,     of this year.
Knee action, Water cooled exhaust.
```

Cullen's letter referred to the birth announcement of Ethel's youngest son, Glenn Ray Nance, created by her first husband, Leroy A. Williams: Private collection of Karen Felecia Nance

Ethel's friendship with Cullen reflected her ability to connect with artists of varied temperaments. She often provided feedback on his work and celebrated his successes. Their shared commitment to fostering literary excellence strengthened Harlem's creative community.

Countee Cullen's formal lyricism and exploration of racial identity set him apart as a Renaissance poet. His works, such as *Color* and *The Ballad of the Brown Girl*, captured the complexities of Black existence with elegance and sensitivity. Ethel's friendship with Cullen highlighted her ability to connect with diverse artistic personalities. She often accompanied him to social events, ensuring he felt included in Harlem's dynamic creative circles.

A Seat at the Table: Ethel Ray Nance & the Harlem Renaissance

Langston Hughes: The Rhythm and Voice of a Movement

Photo: Langston Hughes, Abt 1924, Private collection of Karen Felecia Nance

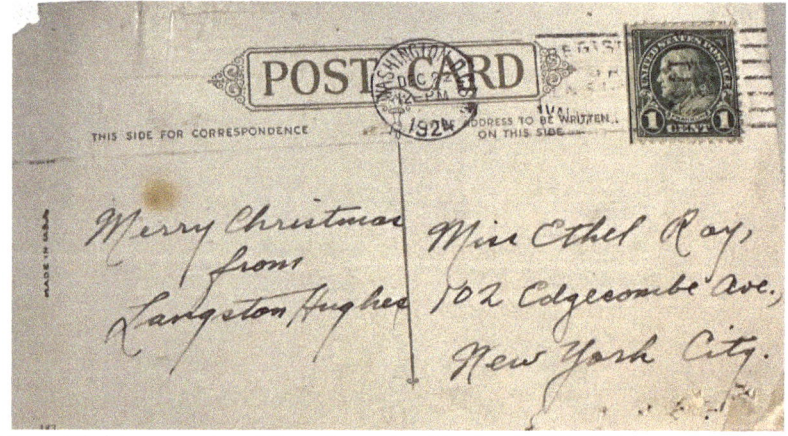

Merry Christmas postcard from Langston Hughes to Ethel Ray postmarked December 22, 1924, Private collection of Karen Felecia Nance

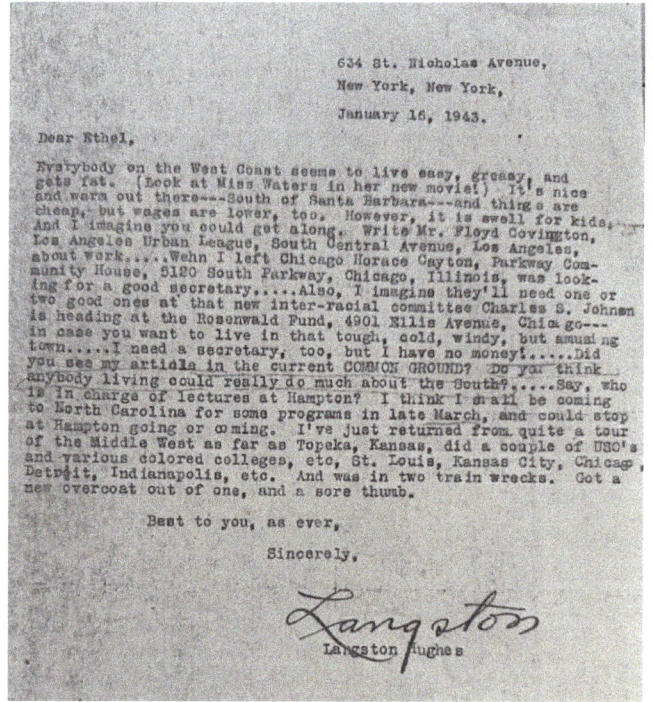

Letter from Langston Hughes to Ethel dated January 16, 1943, Private collection of Karen

A Seat at the Table: Ethel Ray Nance & the Harlem Renaissance

Langston Hughes, known as the "Poet Laureate of Harlem," was one of the most influential voices of the Harlem Renaissance, using his poetry, prose, and plays to capture the spirit, struggles, and triumphs of Black America. His works, including *The Weary Blues*, which won first prize at the Opportunity contest dinner, and *The Negro Speaks of Rivers*, which he wrote at the age of 17, celebrated the resilience of Black life while addressing social and racial injustices. Hughes's ability to connect with people from all walks of life made him a central figure in Harlem's artistic and intellectual circles.

One of the key figures who supported Hughes in his early years was Ethel Ray Nance. Their friendship and collaboration reflected the deep interconnectedness of Harlem's literary and artistic community. Ethel's gatherings at Dream Haven, her home in Harlem, provided Hughes with a space to share his work, engage in spirited discussions, and refine his craft among like-minded artists. Dream Haven became an incubator for Harlem's creative minds, where Hughes, along with other emerging Black intellectuals, could exchange ideas freely.

Ethel played an instrumental role in amplifying Hughes's influence. Recognizing his immense talent, she introduced him to publishers and editors, encouraging him to submit his poetry to *Opportunity*, a publication that was crucial in launching the careers of many Harlem Renaissance writers. Alongside their mutual friend Regina Anderson Andrews, Ethel championed Hughes's work, ensuring that his voice reached a wider audience. Her belief in his artistry was unwavering, and she took pride in witnessing his ascent to literary prominence.

Hughes's frequent visits to Dream Haven underscored the importance of their relationship. The space was a haven for artistic collaboration, where Hughes would share drafts of his poems and engage in lively discussions about the direction of Black literature. One evening, when Hughes was the guest of honor at Dream Haven, he captivated the room with stories of his travels in Europe. Someone inquired whether he had been writing, and in response, he reached into his pocket, pulled out a small notebook, and read his poignant poem:

Life is Fine:

I went down to the river,
I set down on the bank.
I tried to think but couldn't,
So I jumped in and sank.

I came up once and hollered!
I came up twice and cried!
If that water hadn't a-been so cold
I might've sunk and died.

But it was
Cold in that water!
It was cold!

I took the elevator
Sixteen floors above the ground.
I thought about my baby
And thought I would jump down.

I stood there and I hollered!
I stood there and I cried!
If it hadn't a-been so high

A Seat at the Table: Ethel Ray Nance & the Harlem Renaissance

I might've jumped and died.

But it was
High up there!
It was high!

So since I'm still here livin',
I guess I will live on.
I could've died for love—
But for livin' I was born

Though you may hear me holler,
And you may see me cry—
I'll be dogged, sweet baby,
If you gonna see me die.

Life is fine!
Fine as wine!

Life is fine!

The simplicity yet profound depth of these lines left a lasting impression on Ethel and those in attendance. Hughes had a rare gift—he could distill complex emotions into a few verses, making his poetry both accessible and deeply moving. His ability to relate to people from all walks of life was one of the reasons he became such a beloved figure in Harlem. As Ethel observed, "Langston always remained friendly. Everyone liked him. I think that's why he was able to gather all the material for his *Simple* stories. He could stand on a corner; he could converse with anyone on their level."

Ethel and Hughes's friendship was one of mutual respect and intellectual camaraderie. She admired his sharp wit and his ability to capture the essence of Harlem in verse. His poetry, infused with the rhythms of jazz and the vernacular of everyday Black life, broke away from classical forms and embraced the dynamic energy of Harlem's streets, nightclubs, and churches. Hughes's ability to blend the oral traditions of Black America with modernist literary techniques made his work both revolutionary and enduring.

Ethel recorded her reflections on Hughes in her journal, writing:

"Langston Hughes was such a part of Harlem—he loved it. He said in one of his books: 'The sheer size of Harlem intrigues me, partly because poets like James Weldon Johnson and Jessie Fauset lived there. Had I been a rich young man, I would have bought a house and built musical steps up to the front door and installed chimes, which at the press of a button would play Duke Ellington tunes. But I wasn't rich, and I could not live on art and had to go to sea to make a living.'"

This passage encapsulates Hughes's deep connection to Harlem, a city that fueled his artistic inspiration even as financial struggles often forced him to seek work elsewhere. Ethel recognized that Hughes's love for Harlem was not just about its creative energy but also about its people, history, and cultural significance.

Their bond was strengthened by their shared belief in the power of literature to enact change. Through her work at *Opportunity*, Ethel facilitated connections between Hughes and influential literary figures, ensuring that his poetry reached a wider audience. She witnessed firsthand the challenges he faced in a racially divided literary world and remained steadfast in her support.

Beyond their professional relationship, Ethel valued Hughes's friendship and his ability to bring people together. His presence at Dream Haven added to its vibrancy, making it a space where writers, artists, and intellectuals could find encouragement and solidarity. Hughes's work, much like Ethel's advocacy, was deeply rooted in the belief that Black voices deserved to be heard, celebrated, and preserved for future generations.

Hughes's poetry and prose remain some of the most enduring works of the Harlem Renaissance, and Ethel took pride in witnessing his rise to literary prominence. Their relationship exemplified the collaborative spirit of the era—one where artists and intellectuals lifted each other, ensuring that their voices would resonate far beyond Harlem. Through her encouragement, connections, and unwavering support, Ethel played a vital role in shaping the career of one of the greatest poets of the 20th century.

The friendship between Langston Hughes and Ethel Ray Nance serves as a testament to the power of literary and cultural collaboration during the Harlem Renaissance. It was a movement fueled by shared dreams, by artists who believed in the power of their words to challenge, inspire, and transform. And in the heart of it all, Hughes and Nance stood side by side—one a poet, the other a literary advocate—united in their mission to uplift and celebrate Black excellence.

Countie Cullen and Langston Hughes: Poets of the Renaissance

Ethel's friendships with Langston Hughes and Countee Cullen reflected her ability to connect with artists of varied temperaments. Hughes, whose poetry captured the jazz rhythms and struggles of the Black experience, frequently visited Dream Haven to share his work and receive feedback. Ethel's introductions to publishers and collaborators amplified his influence. Cullen, known for his formal lyricism, found a trusted confidante in Ethel, often seeking her literary judgment on his poems.

The Bonds That Shaped a Movement: Ethel Ray Nance & Harlem's Giants

Ethel Ray Nance's relationships with A. Philip Randolph, Alain Locke, Countie Cullen, Arna Bontemps, and Langston Hughes illustrate her indispensable role in the Harlem Renaissance. Whether through personal friendships, professional collaborations, or intellectual exchanges at Dream Haven, Ethel was a key figure in nurturing and supporting some of the movement's most important voices. Her ability to recognize and connect talent helped shape the Renaissance's legacy, ensuring that its literary, artistic, and philosophical contributions would endure for generations.

Through her work at Opportunity, her friendships with leading figures, and her dedication to fostering Black creativity, Ethel Ray Nance stood at the heart of the Harlem Renaissance's intellectual and cultural awakening. Her home provided a space for collaboration, her editorial work helped amplify voices that might have otherwise been overlooked, and her deep friendships with Harlem's greatest minds enriched the movement in ways that continue to resonate in Black literature and history today.

Karen Felecia Nance

Chapter 13: A Voice That Lifted a Nation: James Weldon Johnson's Enduring Legacy

James Weldon Johnson was more than a writer, poet, and civil rights leader; he was a force of nature whose words and activism shaped the landscape of American history. A key figure in the Harlem Renaissance, he used his talents to elevate the voices of Black Americans, advocating for justice through both literature and leadership. Among his many contributions, his most enduring may be the stirring anthem *Lift Every Voice and Sing*, a song that continues to inspire generations and, in today's political climate, resonates with even greater urgency.

For Ethel Ray Nance, James Weldon Johnson was more than just a historical figure; he was someone whose impact was deeply personal. Her father, William Henry Ray, held Johnson's poetry in high regard, often speaking of its brilliance and power. This admiration was instilled in Ethel, shaping her appreciation for literature and justice. Little did she know that her own path would one day cross with Johnson's in the most extraordinary way.

As a researcher for Dr. Charles S. Johnson at *Opportunity Magazine*, Ethel played a vital role in the literary scene of the Harlem Renaissance. In this position, she was entrusted with the significant task of delivering manuscripts to esteemed judges in New York City, one of whom was James Weldon Johnson himself. This was not merely an errand; it was an opportunity to engage with one of the most influential voices in the fight for racial equality. Meeting Johnson in person was an unforgettable experience for Ethel; his intellect, dignity, and commitment to justice left an indelible mark on her.

While Ethel also encountered other notable literary figures such as **Witter Bynner, Dr. Blanche Colton Williams, Dorothy Scarborough,** and **Robert Davis,** none matched the towering presence of James Weldon Johnson. His work was not simply literary; it was revolutionary. He used his voice to advocate for the marginalized, and his contributions went beyond poetry and prose; they helped shape the civil rights movement that would unfold in the decades to come.

At the heart of Johnson's legacy is *Lift Every Voice and Sing*, often called the Negro National Anthem. Originally a poem written in 1900 and later set to music by his brother, John Rosamond Johnson, the song quickly became a rallying cry for hope, resilience, and Black pride. It was first performed by a choir of schoolchildren in Jacksonville, Florida, and soon spread across the country, embraced as an anthem of strength and perseverance in the face of adversity.

Today, *Lift Every Voice and Sing* carries even greater significance. In an era of social unrest, racial reckoning, and political division, its words remind us of both the struggles of the past and the work still ahead. It is a song of defiance against oppression, a hymn of unity in the fight for justice, and a testament to the unbreakable spirit of a people who refuse to be silenced.

Karen Felecia Nance

The powerful lyrics of *Lift Every Voice and Sing* are as relevant today as they were over a century ago:

Lift Every Voice and Sing

By James Weldon Johnson

Lift every voice and sing, till earth and heaven ring,
Ring with the harmonies of Liberty;
Let our rejoicing rise, high as the listening skies,
Let it resound loud as the rolling sea.
Sing a song full of the faith that the dark past has taught us,
Sing a song full of the hope that the present has brought us,
Facing the rising sun of our new day begun,
Let us march on till victory is won.

Stony the road we trod, bitter the chastening rod,
Felt in the days when hope unborn had died;
Yet with a steady beat, have not our weary feet
Come to the place for which our fathers sighed?
We have come over a way that with tears has been watered,
We have come, treading our path through the blood of the slaughtered,
Out from the gloomy past, till now we stand at last
Where the white gleam of our bright star is cast.

God of our weary years, God of our silent tears,
Thou who has brought us thus far on the way;
Thou who has by Thy might led us into the light,

A Seat at the Table: Ethel Ray Nance & the Harlem Renaissance

Keep us forever in the path, we pray.
Lest our feet stray from the places, our God, where we met Thee,
Lest our hearts drunk with the wine of the world, we forget Thee;
Shadowed beneath Thy hand, may we forever stand,
True to our God, true to our native land.

For Ethel Ray Nance, James Weldon Johnson's words and works served as both an inspiration and a call to action. His poetry, leadership, and unwavering commitment to racial justice resonated deeply with her, reinforcing the importance of her own work. Just as *Lift Every Voice and Sing* continues to be sung across generations, so does Johnson's legacy continue to uplift those who strive for justice, equality, and a seat at the table of history.

Chapter 14: Fact or Fiction

Myths and Realities of Ethel Ray Nance and Regina Anderson Andrews

Was Carl Van Vechten's Nigger Heaven Inspired by Real-Life Figures, Including Regina Anderson Andrews and Ethel Ray Nance?

Carl Van Vechten's controversial novel, *Nigger Heaven*, published in 1926, has long been speculated to include characters inspired by real-life figures from the Harlem Renaissance, including Regina Anderson Andrews and Ethel Ray Nance. The book's vivid depiction of Harlem captivated many readers but also provided criticism for its title and racial caricatures, which many in the Black community found offensive and reductive.

Regina Anderson Andrews, known for hosting salons that brought together Harlem's most influential voices, was a cultural curator whose wit, organizational skill, and deep understanding of Harlem's artistic pulse left an indelible mark. Van Vechten's interactions with her likely informed his perceptions of the dynamic figures shaping Harlem at the time.

Ethel Ray Nance, who shared an apartment with Regina, worked closely with W.E.B. Du Bois at *The Crisis* and was deeply involved in civil rights efforts. Her ability to navigate the interconnected worlds of academia, activism, and the arts made her a key figure in Harlem's cultural ecosystem. Ethel had developed a close relationship with Du

A Seat at the Table: Ethel Ray Nance & the Harlem Renaissance

Bois in March 1921 when he visited Duluth, Minnesota, and spoke at St. Mark's AME Church. Their bond, rooted in mutual respect, continued when she moved to New York in May 1924 and began working for Charles S. Johnson, the editor of *Opportunity* magazine.

While there is no concrete evidence that Van Vechten modeled characters in *Nigger Heaven* on Regina or Ethel, the character Mary Love, a sophisticated woman grappling with race and identity, bears striking similarities to the women Van Vechten encountered, including these two trailblazers.

Both Regina and Ethel expressed sharp critiques of *Nigger Heaven*:

Regina Anderson Andrews believed the novel sensationalized Black life and reinforced harmful stereotypes.

Ethel Ray Nance criticized the book for exoticizing Harlem and failing to authentically capture the dignity and richness of Black culture.

Ethel's disapproval of Van Vechten extended beyond the novel. Following the *Opportunity* dinner, she voiced frustration that Charles S. Johnson, a key architect of the event and her employer, received little acknowledgment compared to Van Vechten and other white attendees. This sentiment reflected her broader concerns about white individuals inserting themselves into Harlem's cultural movements without fully respecting their authenticity.

Ethel recalled her unease about Van Vechten's presence: *"I think I had sort of a resentment, maybe not with any certain reason, of white people coming to Harlem. It seemed that we were just being on exhibition, and whenever Mr. Van Vechten came, he usually brought other white people with him."*

Did Ethel Ray Nance Have a Romantic Relationship with W.E.B. Du Bois?

The professional relationship between Ethel Ray Nance and W.E.B. Du Bois was built on mutual respect and collaboration. As Du Bois's stenographer and trusted confidant, Ethel made significant contributions to his work with *The Crisis* and shared his passion for advancing civil rights advocacy. However, in *When Harlem Was in Vogue*, author David Levering Lewis speculates about a possible romantic relationship between Ethel and Du Bois. This claim stems from their close working relationship and shared intellectual interests, yet no substantial evidence supports such speculation.

Ethel and Du Bois addressed each other affectionately as "Marielle" and "André" in letters, but these exchanges lack explicit romantic undertones. The use of these pen names originated from Ethel's father, who found "Ethel" and "William" too ordinary. Seeking a touch of sophistication, he suggested the French names "Marielle" and "André." This influence reflected both his presence in Ethel's life and the family's close relationship with Du Bois. Additionally, neither Ethel's writings nor family recollections suggest romantic involvement, and Du Bois's detailed diaries and letters provide no concrete evidence of such a relationship. Their bond was more likely rooted in mentorship and intellectual camaraderie, with Du Bois, close in age to Ethel's father, William Henry Ray, fostering admiration for her intellect and potential, much as he did for his own daughter.

Ethel wrote:

"The visits of Dr. Du Bois to my parents' home in Minnesota are memorable events in my life," she reflected. *"And I know the visits of Dr. and Mrs. Du Bois to our home in Minneapolis, Hampton, San Francisco, Houston will be as memorable to our sons."*

She spoke of his relentless discipline and the meticulous order of his daily life. "He planned his work by days, weeks, months, and even years in advance," she recalled. "He disliked confusion and permitted no interruptions with his schedule. I did it once! And I never made that mistake again."

Even in her final years, Ethel continued to write, determined to add her perspective to history.

"It's important," she said, *"that the humor and discipline of his life inspire others to carry on his—and my—vision of what life might be."* Then, with a knowing smile, she added, *"I miss him, of course. But I don't really miss his coffee. It was good, mind you, but it wouldn't win any gold medals."*

Speculative Narratives

Speculative narratives, while intriguing, often distract from the substantive achievements of individuals like Ethel Ray Nance and Regina Anderson Andrews. In Ethel's case, rumors about her role in *Nigger Heaven* or a supposed romance with Du Bois risk overshadowing her groundbreaking contributions: serving as the first

Black female police officer in Minnesota, pioneering civil rights advocacy, and acting as a vital cultural connector during the Harlem Renaissance. Similarly, Regina's contributions as a cultural curator and salon host were essential to Harlem's intellectual and artistic scene. These achievements should take precedence over conjecture about their personal lives or potential inspirations for fictional characters.

Speculations about the personal lives of marginalized figures often perpetuate the systemic erasure of their true legacies. While sensational stories might capture attention, they often come at the cost of recognizing the substantive impact these figures had on history. Ethel's relentless advocacy for justice and Regina's role in fostering creativity remain far more significant than the rumors surrounding them. By focusing on their accomplishments, we honor their legacies and ensure their rightful place in history.

Ethel Ray Nance and Regina Anderson Andrews exemplified resilience, innovation, and courage. Their stories highlight the importance of prioritizing documented achievements over speculation, creating a more inclusive and accurate historical narrative. By shifting the focus from rumor to reality, future generations will recognize these women as the trailblazers they were, celebrating their profound impact on civil rights, culture, and the arts.

Chapter 15: "It Felt Like the End of Life": Returning to Duluth

Ethel Ray Nance's return to Minnesota marked a deeply personal and transformative period in her life. Her mother's illness brought her back to Duluth, a homecoming that felt like the end of life as she had known it. Leaving Harlem, the epicenter of cultural and intellectual awakening, was not an easy decision, but familial duty prevailed.

Ethel with her mother, Inga, after returning home from New York. Photo taken after 1926, Private collection of Karen Felecia Nance

Enroute home from New York
October 19, 1925

There is nothing virile about the appearance of the scattered clumps of trees in Ohio - especially in their fall garb they seem products of a dying civilization, - civilized to the degree of rapid extinction.

In Minnesota the fiery reds and warm browns and lively yellows suggest efferescent life - it arouses the savage spirit of conquest within one - here is something still barbaric, untamed, defying man's puny jurisdiction. The general contour of Ohio and this vicinity suggests submission, submission to conventions - contentment to be nicely rounded off into graceful forms that are surely monotonous, - no rude independent branches shooting out unexpectedly in any direction which add individual beauty and make one turn around to hold the unusualness as long as the eye can see it, and make one hunger greedily for the next wild, crazy exhibition of the carefree spirit of the untamed.

- - - - - - -

Hills appear out of the mist without warning -

The darkness and heaviness of the day make one listless toward effort.......

Possibly the hills are imaginary, existing in my mind only - but it's a good setting for them in these low valleys of Pennsylvania. ...

Great blotches of cloud are covering the warm blue sky in varying shades of gray and thicknesses, overlapping.... not light and feathery but powerful, suggesting a strength capable of suffocation - it would crush out any life slowly, relentlessly, but surely, whatever at - tempted to hinder its swiftly moving body....

Out of the window I see clumps of gray-tan weeds hovering together like miniature grazing sheep..

Ethel's diary entry dated October 19, 1925. Private collection of Karen Felecia Nance.

A Seat at the Table: Ethel Ray Nance & the Harlem Renaissance

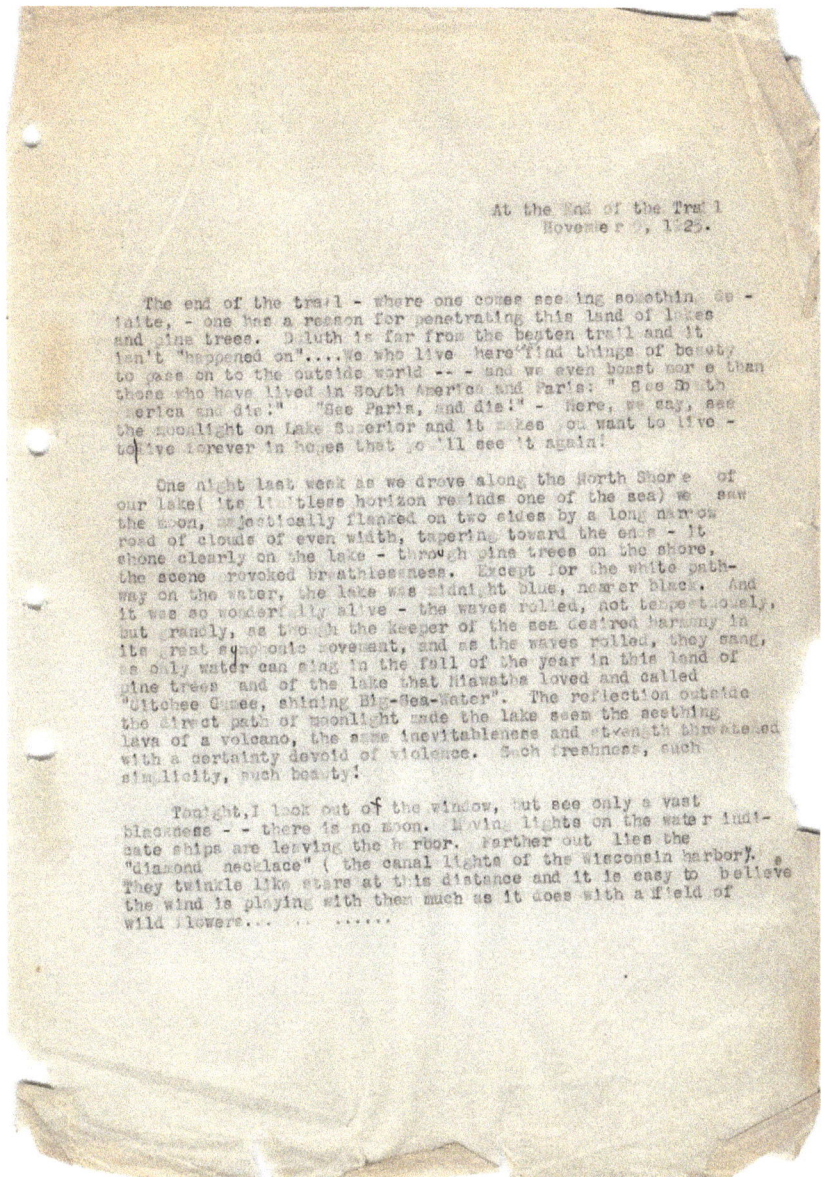

Ethel's diary entry dated November 9, 1925. Private collection of Karen Felecia Nance

"My mother's illness brought me back to Minnesota—which felt like the end of life for me," Ethel wrote. "Any improvement in her health condition reversed itself when I talked of returning East." The suffocating stillness of home contrasted sharply with the vibrant energy she had left behind. "My periods of depression, constantly looking for and receiving mail from New York, kept the atmosphere in the house nearly unbearable for all."

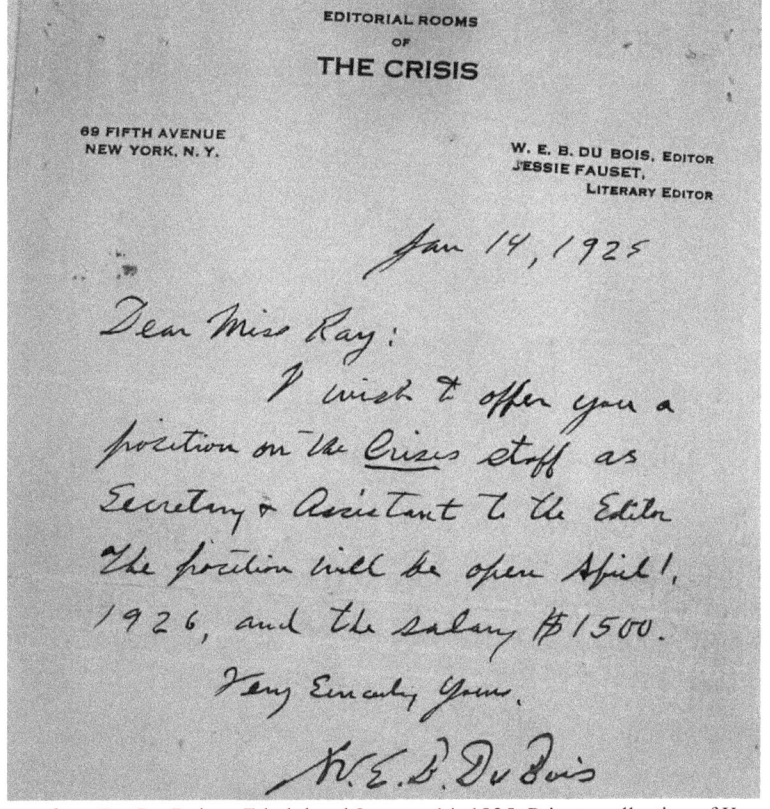

Letter from Dr. Du Bois to Ethel dated January 14, 1925. Private collection of Karen Felecia

A Seat at the Table: Ethel Ray Nance & the Harlem Renaissance

> Now I was in a dilemma. I wanted to go back to New York, regardless of where I worked - just to get back. My father felt I should write Opportunity Magazine and tell them of the improvement in my mother's health, that I could return to New York, and I should also mention the offer from the Crisis Magazine.
>
> I did so. Charles Johnson answered immediately, saying after my letter reached him saying I could not return for at least a year, they had hired someone for that period. He also said he could not ask me to refuse the Crisis offer, but that he feared it might develop into a definite break with Opportunity since after a year I would become rather firmly entrenched in that magazine. He also said that "he hoped I would still consider myself a part of Opportunity, and my loyalty would remain there."
>
> My father said the situation was a hard one to resolve, and one I would have to come to a decision on myself. A few sleepless nights followed, in thoughts becoming circles, winding and unwinding. I wanted to return to New York so badly, but the word "loyalty" that Johnson used rather stumped me. If I hadn't been in my twenties my decision would not have been so difficult. (Years later when I had the opportunity to talk with Johnson about my decision I told him, he was definitely playing on my inexperience and naivety, and I felt he asked me to make an impossible promise of "loyalty". He laughed, and said: "You know, young lady, anything's fair in war..." He could be ruthless when the occasion arose.)
>
> There seemed no alternative but to answer the Crisis letter of January 14th, saying I could not return "just then."

Ethel's undated diary entry discussing her dilemma (1925). Private collection of Karen

In December 1925, Ethel accepted a position as a stenographer in Duluth at the District Auto License Registration Department, working for her former employer, H.V. Eva. She remained there until April 1926, when she moved to Minneapolis to work at the Phyllis Wheatley Settlement House. Surrounded by young people, she found comfort in an environment that provided a buffer between herself and the outside world.

Despite her best efforts to settle into this new chapter, Harlem still called to her. She had spent less than two years in New York, but those years had been filled with purpose, creativity, and community. She later reflected on her decision to leave:

"You have to look at things as they come."

When Ethel's mother's health improved, Ethel considered returning to Harlem. Her father warned her:

"You would be 1500 miles away from home, and if anything happens to your mother, you'll always regret all your life that you were so far away."

Torn between obligation and ambition, she remained in Minnesota, but she was not happy.

Her mother noticed and urged her to go back:

"When you are home and receive mail, you are sad, and if you do not get mail, you are sad."

Determined to return, Ethel packed her bags and wrote to Charles S. Johnson, informing him that she was ready to return. But just a week earlier, she had written him a letter stating she needed to stay home for at least a year. By the time Johnson received her second letter, he had already hired someone else.

Shortly after, W.E.B. Du Bois offered her a position at *The Crisis* office, an opportunity she desperately wanted. But in an act of youthful honesty, she wrote to Johnson for guidance. His response was measured but clear; he hoped her loyalty remained with *Opportunity,* and he subtly cautioned against bringing their shared plans to *The Crisis.* At the time, The Crisis was hosting a literary contest, and Johnson worried about the overlap between the two publications.

Seeking further counsel, Ethel turned to her father, who simply said:

"It is up to you to make your decision, but it would be difficult if you went."

And so, she stayed.

Later, she reflected:

"I only wished there had been someone who could have advised me to have gone back."

Sustaining the Spirit of Harlem

Though Harlem seemed out of reach, Ethel refused to let go of its spirit. She channeled the energy of the Harlem Renaissance into her community, organizing book clubs, volunteering with civil rights groups, and founding historical societies that celebrated Black achievements. She maintained correspondence with the intellectuals she had left behind, continuing to support the movement from afar.

Her diary entries from this period reveal her longing for Harlem's intellectual vibrancy:

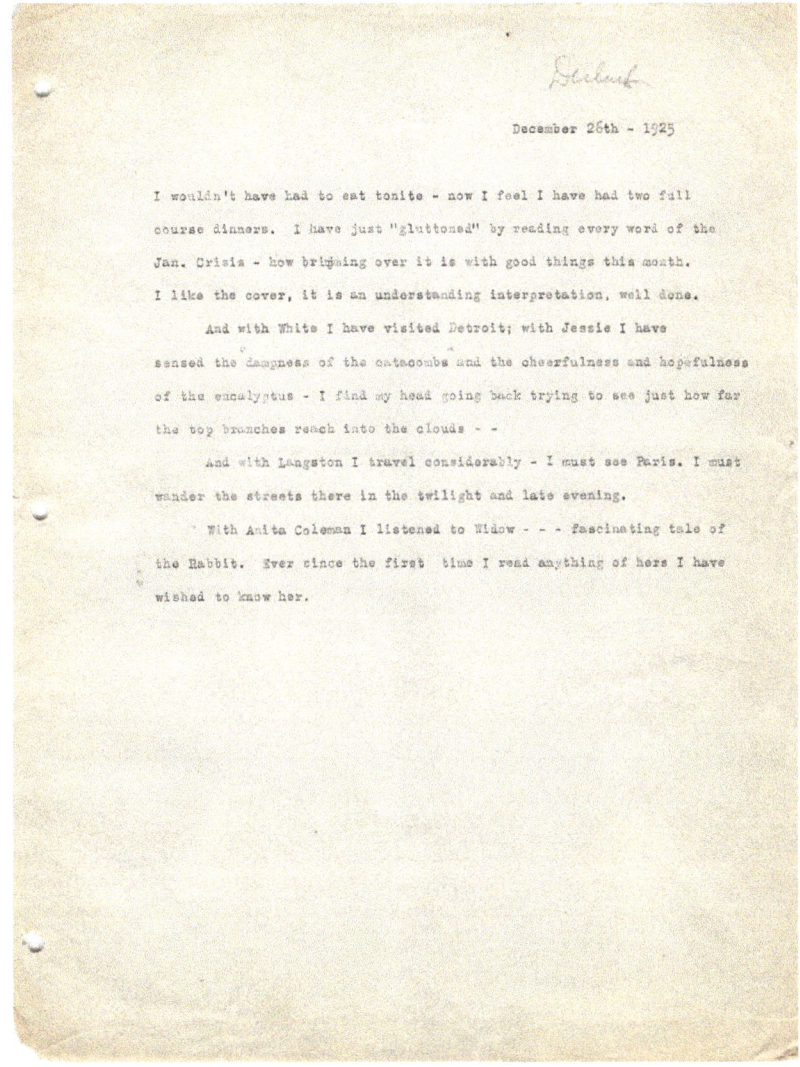

Ethel's December 26, 1925, diary entry. Private collection of Karen Felecia Nance

Although physically removed from Harlem, she never stopped dreaming about the world she had briefly inhabited.

Karen Felecia Nance

The Apollo Theatre: A Legacy of Performance and Power

During her time in Harlem, Ethel Ray Nance witnessed the rise of the Apollo Theatre, a venue that would become the beating heart of Black entertainment in America. While the Apollo officially opened its doors to Black audiences and performers in 1934, it had already begun to carve out a space for Black artistry and cultural expression during the Harlem Renaissance.

Figures like Billie Holiday, Ella Fitzgerald, and Duke Ellington would go on to transform Apollo into an international icon, but for Ethel and her peers, the theater was more than just a stage; it was a symbol of possibility. It represented the realization of Black excellence, a place where talent was nurtured, voices were amplified, and cultural identity was celebrated.

Even after leaving Harlem, Ethel followed the careers of Apollo performers, keeping in touch with the movement's evolution through magazines like *The Crisis* and *Opportunity*. She understood that, just as Harlem had become a literary and artistic capital, the Apollo had become a proving ground for Black performers, cementing their place in American history.

Though she could not have known it at the time, the Apollo Theatre would go on to shape the careers of James Brown, Aretha Franklin, and The Jackson 5, ensuring that Harlem's influence on Black culture extended far beyond its initial Renaissance years.

The Edge Harlem: A Living Tribute

In 2024, The Edge Harlem celebrated its 10th anniversary. This restaurant, owned and operated by sisters Justine and Juliet Masters, is located in the very building where Ethel once lived with Regina Anderson Andrews and Louella Tucker, a home they affectionately called "Dream Haven."

During the Harlem Renaissance, Dream Haven was more than just a residence; it was a gathering place for intellectuals, artists, and visionaries, fostering the very creativity that defined the era. The Edge Harlem pays homage to this legacy, blending its rich history with modern vibrancy.

With a menu inspired by global flavors, a welcoming atmosphere, and a deep respect for Harlem's cultural heritage, The Edge Harlem has become a bridge between past and present. Its walls are adorned with photographs and memorabilia that celebrate Harlem's storied history, including the iconic group photo taken after the Opportunity Dinner in 1925.

In 2022, I had the privilege of visiting The Edge Harlem and meeting Justine and Juliet Masters. As I explored the restaurant, I was thrilled to discover the very group photo from March 21, 1925, prominently displayed. Seeing my grandmother, Ethel Ray Nance, among luminaries like Langston Hughes, Regina Anderson Andrews, and Rudolph Fisher was a deeply moving experience.

It was a poignant reminder of her role in shaping the Renaissance and her enduring presence in Harlem's history.

Juliet Master, Karen Nance, Justine Master, The Edge Harlem Restaurant, 2022, Private collection of Karen Felecia Nance

    The Edge Harlem's 10th anniversary symbolizes the continuity of Harlem's cultural significance. Just as Dream Haven was a space for collaboration and inspiration, The Edge Harlem continues to be a gathering place that celebrates the spirit of community and creativity.

Part V: A Legacy That Lives On

Chapter 16. The Power of Symbolism and Legacy

The convergence of these landmark anniversaries in 2024, Ethel's 125th birthday, the 90th anniversary of the Apollo Theatre, and the 10th anniversary of The Edge Harlem restaurant, and in 2025, the 100th Anniversary of the Opportunity Dinner, offers a rare opportunity to reflect on the interconnectedness of history.

Together, these milestones underscore the enduring influence of individuals and movements that have shaped the fight for justice, equality, and cultural empowerment.

Ethel's journey—from Duluth to Harlem and beyond—exemplifies the resilience required to navigate the complexities of race, gender, and identity. Her unwavering dedication to preserving history reminds us that the past is never truly behind us; it continues to shape the present and inform the future.

The Opportunity Dinner's centennial serves as a powerful reminder of the transformative power of community, while The Edge Harlem's ongoing presence as a cultural hub emphasizes the importance of preserving and celebrating history in real time.

These anniversaries also invite us to consider the broader significance of the Harlem Renaissance, a movement that redefined Black identity, artistry, and activism. It was a time when writers, musicians, and social leaders came together to challenge stereotypes, demand justice, and create a new narrative for Black America—ideals that remain as vital today as they were a century ago.

Chapter 17: A Call to Action for Future Generations

As we honor the legacy of Ethel Ray Nance and the Harlem Renaissance, we are reminded that the work they began is far from finished. The fight for justice, equality, and representation continues, and the lessons of the past serve as invaluable guideposts for the future.

The celebrations in 2024 and 2025 are not just commemorations; they are a call to action. They urge us to carry forward the spirit of resilience, creativity, and activism embodied by Ethel and her contemporaries.

Whether through storytelling, community-building, or advocacy, each of us has a role to play in ensuring that our legacy continues to inspire change.

The Edge Harlem stands as a beacon of hope and inspiration, a living testament to the power of place to connect generations and foster transformation. As visitors gather beneath the photograph of Ethel and her peers, they are invited to reflect on the legacy of the Harlem Renaissance and the ongoing importance of community, collaboration, and courage.

The story of Ethel Ray Nance is not just about the past—it is about what comes next.

Epilogue

Ethel Ray Nance understood the power of history—and, more importantly, the responsibility to preserve it.

She once said:

"People who wish their point of view presented must leave their own record for future historians to read."

These words are more than just a personal reflection. They are a challenge to all of us.

Throughout her lifetime, Ethel made it her mission to ensure that Black voices, stories, and achievements were not erased or overlooked. Whether through her groundbreaking work at *Opportunity* magazine, her collaborations with W.E.B. Du Bois, her friendships with Langston Hughes, Countee Cullen, and Alain Locke, or her role as Minnesota's first Black policewoman, she dedicated herself to documenting history as it unfolded.

She knew that storytelling was more than just a means of expression; it was a tool for empowerment, justice, and cultural continuity.

Ethel's journey from Duluth to Harlem and back again was not just a geographic one; it was a passage through some of the most defining moments of the 20th century. She stood at the crossroads of cultural renaissance and social transformation, playing a pivotal role in bridging communities, amplifying voices, and facilitating change.

Her friendships and professional relationships with writers, activists, and intellectuals exemplified the collaborative spirit of the Harlem Renaissance, where individuals uplifted one another to create a lasting impact.

Her departure from Harlem did not mark the end of her influence; it simply signified a shift. Her work in Kansas City, Missouri, Minnesota, Nashville, and San Francisco ensured that her legacy extended beyond Harlem's boundaries. Though she at times questioned her decision to leave Harlem and to care for her mother in Duluth, her commitment to community-building, historical preservation, and justice never wavered.

Today, Ethel Ray Nance's contributions are finally receiving the recognition they deserve. With the declaration of Ethel Ray Nance Day in Duluth, the publications of works that highlight her achievements, and ongoing efforts to elevate her story, her impact is no longer hidden in the margins of history—it is taking center stage.

Her words remind us that history is not only written by the powerful; it is also shaped by those who take the time to record their experiences.

This book, in its entirety, is a testament to that philosophy. It is a continuation of the record that Ethel herself sought to leave, a narrative of resilience, artistry, activism, and an unwavering commitment to justice.

As we close this chapter of Ethel Ray Nance's life and legacy, her words continue to resonate. They challenge us to document our own histories, to uplift the voices of the marginalized, and to honor those who came before us by preserving their truths. This book offers only a sliver of her extraordinary journey—there is much more to uncover, share, and celebrate. Her story does not end here; it continues to inspire, shape conversations, and guide future generations in the pursuit of justice, creativity, and historic preservation.

Her life serves as a reminder that every voice matters, every story is valuable, and every record left behind helps shape the world that future historians will come to understand.

The Harlem Renaissance was more than just a cultural movement—it was a declaration of identity, a reclaiming of history, and an assertion of Black excellence in literature, art, and activism.

And within that movement, Ethel Ray Nance stood as a crucial force—not only helping to make history but ensuring that it would never be forgotten.

Her legacy endures in the records she helped create, in the connections she forged, and in the lives she touched.

In honoring her, we reaffirm the truth of her own words:

"People who wish their point of view presented must leave their own record for future historians to read."

About the Author

Karen Felecia Nance is an author, attorney, mediator, private investigator, and advocate whose work centers on justice, equality, and historic preservation. Through her writing, she sheds light on the extraordinary contributions of **Ethel Ray Nance** and other trailblazers who have shaped the fight for civil rights and social progress.

Karen has published the following works:

1. *My Father Poisoned Me, Or Did He?*

    A compelling memoir that delves into family, identity, and truth-seeking, exploring personal and historical narratives with depth and introspection.

2. *Ethel Ray Nance: Living in the White, Gray, and Black*

    A powerful biography that chronicles Ethel Ray Nance's groundbreaking work in civil rights, law enforcement, and racial inequities. This book highlights Nance's role in documenting Black history and fostering cross-cultural understanding.

3. *From Ethel Ray Nance to Kamala Harris: A Legacy of Equality and Justice*

This work bridges historical and contemporary struggles for racial and gender equality, drawing a line from **Ethel Ray Nance's activism to the rise of Kamala Harris**, the first woman and first Black and South Asian Vice President of the United States.

Through her writing, **Karen Felecia Nance** preserves and amplifies the legacy of **Ethel Ray Nance**, ensuring that her impact on civil rights, literature, and social justice remains recognized and celebrated. These books represent only a sliver of the rich history she is committed to uncovering, with much more to come.

Karen continues to advocate for historical truth, intersectional justice, and community empowerment, using her platform to connect past struggles with present-day activism.